"With refreshing candor and careful re. answers the questions most often posed about the Christian faith. If you are a skeptic, a cynic, or among the curious, you will find a friend in this book, a friend who understands your questions and offers answers that satisfy head and heart."

—*Chuck Colson*,
founder, Prison Fellowship

"A brilliant book by an outstanding teacher and evangelist. *Avoiding Jesus* is a must for all of us who wish to reach the hearts and minds of people today."

—*George Carey*,
former Archbishop of Canterbury

"This is an outstanding book—a sympathetic, honest, and thorough examination of contemporary objections to Christian belief. Michael Green is one of the world's foremost Christian communicators, and this book will delight its many readers."

—*Alister McGrath*,
professor of historical theology, Oxford University;
director, Oxford Centre for Evangelism and Apologetics

Avoiding Jesus

*Answers for Skeptics, Cynics,
and the Curious*

Michael Green

BakerBooks
Grand Rapids, Michigan

Published in the USA in 2005 by Baker Books
a division of Baker Publishing Group
P.O. Box 6287, Grand Rapids, MI 49516-6287
www.bakerbooks.com

Originally published by Sovereign World Limited of Tonbridge, Kent, England

Printed in the United States of America

Library of Congress Cataloging-in-Publication Data

Green, Michael, 1930-
    Avoiding Jesus : answers to skeptics, cynics, and the curious / Michael
Green.
        p. cm.
    Includes bibliographical references (p.   ).
    ISBN 0-8010-6561-5 (pbk.)
    1. Jesus Christ. 2. Apologetics. I. Title.

BT1212.G74 2005
239—dc22

2005041126

Unless otherwise indicated, Scripture is taken from the Revised Standard
Version of the Bible, copyright 1952 [2nd edition, 1971] by the Division of
Christian Education of the National Council of the Churches of Christ in the
United States of America. Used by permission. All rights reserved.

Scripture marked NIV is taken from the HOLY BIBLE, NEW INTERNATIONAL
VERSION®. NIV®. Copyright © 1973, 1978, 1984 by International Bible
Society. Used by permission of Zondervan. All rights reserved.

Scripture marked NLT is taken from the *Holy Bible*, New Living Translation,
copyright © 1996. Used by permission of Tyndale House Publishers, Inc.,
Wheaton, Illinois 60189. All rights reserved.

Contents

Thank you...

The stimulus to write this sort of book came from Friedrich Hänssler, the head of Hänssler-Verlag Publishing. The idea and original title emerged as I lay in Durban Hospital with meningitis, under the care and imaginative friendship of Dr. John Hill. The chapter headings came from the many people who have tried them out on me! The original book, *You Must Be Joking*, published in 1976, has been read worldwide in repeated editions and scores of languages. When Hodder and Stoughton relinquished the title in 2003, four other publishers immediately asked me to republish it.

I do so now after radical revision and with the addition of several new chapters. Valuable suggestions came from Tony Collins of Monarch and Chris Mungeam of Sovereign World. To one and all, thank you.

Michael Green

1

From the Author ...

If I had titled this chapter "Foreword" or "Preface," you would possibly have skipped it. But I want you to read it. It is quite important, and it shows what the book is about.

A startling agreement ...

I have had the opportunity of traveling widely in Europe, Asia, Africa, North America, and Australia. I have had the chance to discover the basic attitudes to life adopted by ordinary people of every conceivable variety of background, color, and education. You would expect these attitudes to differ enormously, and on most subjects, of course, they do. But on one subject there is startling agreement. When it is a matter of what men and women think about human nature and religion, our origin and destiny, the possibility of forgiveness, or life after death— then people tend to come up with the same answers, whether they hail from San Francisco or Sydney. Such agreement looks, at first sight, to be very encouraging: when the United Nations can rarely agree about anything at all, it is amazing that people all over the world should tend to think alike about the basic questions of our existence. However, I am not very impressed by this apparent unanimity.

... but shallow

For one thing, it is shallow. When you broach the questions of religion, and someone replies, "Oh, but all religions lead to

God," ten to one he knows almost nothing about his own religious background, still less about any other. When he says, "I'm not the religious kind," you can be fairly confident that he has made no investigation whatever into whether or not there is a religious kind, and, if there is, what it is like. When he says, "Jesus was just a marvelous teacher, but no more," it is unusual to find that he has ever examined the claims Jesus made, or the evidence supporting those claims. When you hear a person say, "I do my best—no one can do more," of one thing you can be certain: he does not do his best (which of us does?) but he hasn't the honesty to admit as much. So do you see why I am not all that impressed by these excuses that come up regularly whenever I begin to talk about God? They are so shallow. They simply show that people, on the whole, are content not to *think* about the really important matters of life and death. "Oh, I have no time for religion," says a prosperous business executive who spends an hour a day keeping up with the stock market. But if there is a God, if there is a heaven, if there is forgiveness, what an appallingly short-sighted attitude! The person who invests shrewdly and carefully in stocks and shares may be pathetically naive and incompetent when it comes to investing in life.

. . . and escapist

There's another reason why I am not impressed by the common responses about religion, which I meet everywhere I go. They are not only shallow, betraying an absence of thought; they are also evasive, betraying an unwillingness to face up to the evidence. Many of the things people come out with, when you ask them their fundamental attitudes toward life, boil down to something like the answers I examine in the chapters that follow. And the trouble is that they are not only shallow but dishonest. Those who say, "It doesn't matter what you believe as long as you are sincere," would never dream of applying that motto to any area of life other than religion. They may think they're being straightforward when they come out with a statement like this, but they aren't really. What they mean is that they are not going to take the trouble to investigate the truth of Christianity or of any other religion— maybe because they don't think it's important enough, maybe because they fear they would be exposed or challenged or become involved. Although it sounds so fine and liberal minded, a person like that is an escapist at heart.

You see, then, why I am not satisfied to find such widespread agreement about fundamental beliefs? The agreement is unthinking and escapist. It is an agnosticism that does not want to know, in case the answer should prove costly or inconvenient. So right at the outset of this little book, I am going to ask you to be different.

A plea for honesty

Will you stand out from the crowd and think for yourself? Will you have the courage to examine the evidence and ask yourself how sound are the assumptions about God and meaning, life and death, with which you have lived so far? Will they bear the weight of your life and future? After all, these *are* the basic issues. It makes an enormous difference if there is a God or not; if he has revealed himself or not; if he will accept us or not; whether we have a future after death or not. It simply will not do to hide our heads in the sand, repeat our excuses, and refuse to see how they stand up to critical examination. The Old Testament has some vivid things to say about people who "have made lies [their] refuge" and how "hail will sweep away the refuge of lies" (Isa. 28:15, 17). Could your refuge be like that? A famous insurance company had, as one of its sales gimmicks, the picture of a roof and the phrase "Refuge for Life." Well, have you got a roof that will keep the rain out? The New Testament (Matt. 7:24–27) records the contrast between the man who built the house of his life on the rock and the one who built on sand. The rain and the wind and the floods assail both houses, but only the house on the rock can withstand the onslaught. Could it be that you are building on sand?

The following chapters discuss a number of very common assumptions about the most important issues in life or objections to Christianity. You may recognize one or more of these statements, even agree with them. If you do, why not begin with that chapter, and ask yourself if the assumption is well founded—or mistaken? Let me, for my part, come clean at the outset. To my mind these assumptions sound good, but they won't do. They are dangerous fallacies and offer no proper foundation for life. Time and again, when people have brought them forward, I have felt (or said!), "You can't be serious!" Will you too come clean at the outset? Lay aside prejudice; examine the evidence; and be prepared for change, should you become persuaded that your assumptions don't hold water. These matters are of critical importance to all of us. There really is no excuse for shallow thinking or evasive action as we look at them together.

2

"I'm not the religious kind."

The religious kind

"No, Pastor, go and talk to someone else. I'm afraid I'm not the religious kind." That is very often said, and I have a lot of sympathy with it. There is something creepy and sanctimonious, something effeminate and wet about that phrase "the religious kind." I think of business people in black suits at the funeral of one of their friends, trying to imitate "the religious kind" for half an hour, and then emerging breathless from the funeral to the open air in order to light a cigarette and return to normality. Or take two very different examples of "religion." One comes on the radio with the daily service and a handful of singers who may sound professional and bogus; canned religion is not attractive at the best of times. The other comes in a great stadium where the evangelist is urging people to come to the front for counseling; that can seem a mere playing on the religious emotions—and "I'm not the religious kind."

Hypocrisy

Why do we so strongly dislike "the religious kind"? Is it not because we have almost come to regard religion and hypocrisy as the same thing? There is a very long history of this. In Isaiah's day back in the eighth century BC, men and women were offering God all kinds of sacrifices, but their hearts were far from him. In Jesus's day, the scribes and Pharisees gained the reputation for being hypocrites. Many of them must have been absolutely genuine. Some, however, were seen to pray long prayers in order to impress; to give ostentatiously so that everyone would see how generous they were; to make a great show of their biblical knowledge in order to shame others. Piety outside and corruption inside is a revolting mixture. Jesus had to accuse some of his hearers of being just like that; they reminded him of the white sepulchers that were such a common sight on the hills, set against the deep blue of the Sea of Galilee. They looked marvelous from the outside, but inside they were foul and full of corruption and dead men's bones.

The link between religion and hypocrisy did not die in the first century. Think of the hypocrisy in those very religious days of the Victorian era: the immorality that flourished, the exploitation that went on alongside meticulous religious observance. And, rightly or wrongly, there are many who suspect hypocrisy in the high churchgoing figures among the middle class in America. God for an hour on Sunday maybe, but where is he on Monday? One thing I am very clear about. Many people assert very forcefully that they are not the religious kind because they hate hypocrisy, and they feel that somehow it is tied up with religion.

Begging?

Closely allied to hypocrisy is begging. None of us like seeing beggars. It makes us feel uncomfortable; indeed, we feel put upon. But organized religion bears the image of the beggar. How many churches do you pass with a notice outside inviting you to restore this historic building? How many cathedrals do you go into with a notice inside telling you how much per minute it costs to run the place?

I understand the effect of all this. Indeed, that is why I said at the outset that I have a lot of sympathy with people who say they are not the religious kind. But all the same I think they are wrong.

Clearing the air

First, let me clear the air and have a look at those justifiable objections to the religious kind that have just been raised. It is true that a lot of bad things have been done in the name of religion. Bad things have also been done in the name of medicine, but that does not mean we never go near a doctor. A lot of good things have been done in the name of religion too, but that fact by itself does not make religion true. There is only one proper question for people of integrity: is the Christian account of the world and humanity true? If it is, then I want it, however many bad things have been sheltered under its umbrella. I want to throw the bad things out into the rain but not take down the umbrella.

It is perfectly true that some expressions of religion border on the nauseating, but what is nauseating to one person is meat and drink to another. I personally get turned off very fast by chanted services in cathedrals. Others get annoyed by prayer meetings, evangelistic rallies, or good old gospel singing. I have no doubt that there is a great deal of insincerity in church circles, and I have no doubt that illicit psychological pressure is exerted by some evangelists. But once again, back to the basic facts. Was Jesus, or was he not, the Son of God? Did he, or did he not, rise from the dead? If he did, then I can afford to be broad-minded about the types of religious expression I personally dislike. If not, then all of it is nonsense, a type of escapism for which I have no time.

As for hypocrisy and money-grabbing, these need not detain us long. Just because there are counterfeit coins about, that does not stop you from using money, does it? Indeed, if there was no "good" money, nobody would bother making counterfeit bills. So the existence of hypocrisy in religious circles is no reason for rejecting religion. Rather it suggests that there is a genuine article as well as numerous forgeries. Take a good hard look at Jesus in the Gospels. There is not a hint of hypocrisy about him. He was the first to denounce it in others. And it is with Jesus that we are concerned. Following him means following the one who denounced hypocrisy and would have no part in it at all. Just because some of his followers have failed to live up to that should not stop you from giving it a try.

On the money-grabbing issue, I think the church has deserved its appalling image. It does give the impression that it is always out for money. The church should proclaim that it has found great treasure in Jesus Christ and that, unlike most treasures, this one is to be given away free. Jesus was always impressing upon people that entry into the kingdom of God, or the Great Supper, or friendship with himself (all three add up to the same thing) was absolutely free—for black and white, Jew and Gentile, prostitute and Pharisee alike. Free. Don't let the church prevent you from discovering the most wonderful person in the world, Jesus himself.

Having, I hope, cleared the air, I now want to ask some pertinent questions of any who are hiding behind this "I'm not the religious kind" motto.

Is there a religious kind?

First, let me ask you, *can you honestly say there is such a thing as a "religious kind"*? Don't pretend it is comprised of the effeminate, the aged, and the dim-witted. I think about some of the people in the Oxford church I used to serve: a leading gynecologist, a factory worker, a librarian, a horticulturist, a garage owner, a builder, an architect, an engineer, a man who began his Christian life in prison, a lawyer, an atomic scientist, a university professor, someone on the dole, hundreds of students, the majority of whom were studying scientific subjects, members from Iran and India, Sri Lanka and South Africa (black and white), the United States, Canada and Sweden, Germany and Hong Kong, Japan and Australia, Kenya and Uganda, Sudan and Nigeria, and so on. The diversity of their attitudes, their backgrounds, their educational achievements, their temperaments, their ages, their interests, their *everything* was so vast that it would be ridiculous to class them all as the religious type. Christians are not just one type: they are all types—extrovert and introvert, tough and weak, old and young, black and white. Their diversity has only one unifying factor, but that factor—Jesus Christ—is strong as steel.

Can you say that the first disciples of Jesus were the religious kind? Perhaps a mystic like John was, but what of rugged, hard-working fishermen like Andrew and Peter? What of freedom fighters like Judas Iscariot and Simon the Zealot? What of money-grabbing tax collectors like Matthew? What of the drunkards and sexual perverts at Corinth who became Christians? What of the thieves and magicians at Ephesus? It is ludicrous to suppose that the people who first followed Jesus belonged to the religious kind. The Jews, in fact, had a word for the religious kind, and another far from complimentary word for the ordinary folk, "the people of the land." All Jesus's first followers came from this latter group: all were the nonreligious kind.

A nonreligious faith

Don't let your dislike of religion keep you away from Jesus. In a very real sense he came to destroy religion. The German martyr Dietrich Bonhoeffer was not playing with words when he coined the phrase "religionless Christianity." That is precisely what Christianity is. It is not an attempt by virtuous men and women to please God and win a place in heaven. It is God coming in his love and generosity to seek folk who would never seek him, holding out his arms to them on a cross and saying, "Come to me, and let us share life together." Not a religion but a rescue. That is why the earliest Christians were so keen to stress that they had no temple, no altars, no priests. They had no religion in the normally accepted sense of the term; hence the Romans called them "atheists." Instead they had a person, who knew them, loved them, and never left them. Nothing could separate them from his loving presence. So prayer became not a ritual but conversation with a friend. Worship was not a ceremony for Sundays but the natural outpouring of love and adoration to the Savior by his people when they met together. They needed no churches, for where two or three were gathered together in his name, he was in their midst. They needed no priests, for Jesus had opened immediate, equal access to God's presence for every one of them. Christianity, properly understood, is the earthiest of faiths; it does not separate the secular from the sacred but keeps the two firmly together. The Lord is as interested in what I do at eleven o'clock on Monday morning in my daily work as he is in what I do at eleven o'clock on Sunday in a church service.

Yes, Christianity is for nonreligious people. It is not going too far to say that if you insist on being religious, you will find Christianity hard, almost impossible. You will find it almost impossible to *become* a Christian, because your "religion" will get in the way: you will feel that somehow you are better and more pleasing to God than your irreligious neighbor, which is exactly what the Pharisees felt—and what kept them away from Jesus. And you will find it almost impossible to *be* a Christian, because once again your "religion" will get in the way: you will feel that the Christian life depends on your religious observances, and not on the Lord. You will be inclined to keep a little religious corner in your life for God and not allow him to have the whole thing. You will definitely find it much harder to become and to be a Christian than the person who is not "the religious kind."

The matter of truth

And now a few other questions for the man or woman who is not religious. *Are you concerned about truth?* That is a vital question. Do I hear you say, "Of course I am"? Okay, then you and the Christian are interested in just the same thing.

Jesus claimed, "I am ... the truth" (John 14:6). He claimed, in other words, to be the ultimate reality in personal, human terms. If you are interested in what is ultimate and what is real, then you cannot remain disinterested in Jesus. You may examine his claims and dismiss them as untrue. What you cannot do, if you maintain a deep concern for truth, is to pay him no attention, shrug your shoulders and say, "I'm not the religious kind."

The matter of courage

Next question: *have you the courage of your convictions?* I once met an atheist at a discussion group, an able man doing doctoral studies in physics. When we were talking personally at the end of the meeting, I asked him if he had ever read one of the Gospels with an open mind, willing to respond to Christ if and when he was convinced by what he read. His reply surprised me, but on reflection I think it may be true of many others. He said, "I dare not." What a remarkable admission! Here was a man used to assessing material, making judgments, committing himself to theories in physics on the ground of the evidence; yet he was afraid to do the same with the New Testament in case it should convince him and draw him to the Christ he was evading. Surely, if he had the courage of his atheistic convictions, he should have been quite willing to read the Gospels. It would give him firsthand material to use in mocking his believing friends. But no. He did not have the courage of his convictions.

The matter of cost

The next question is very similar: *dare you take your stand with a minority?* Jesus warned potential disciples to sit down and count the cost of what following him would mean. Were they prepared to stand with ten thousand men against an opposing force of twenty thousand? If not, they would have to make humiliating peace terms in double-quick time. It is not pleasant to admit you are wrong about the basic issues of life and death. Not easy to join the despised Christian company. Not easy to tolerate being mocked at work for your allegiance to Christ. Not easy to allow Christ to affect your morality. Of course it isn't. Jesus never said it would be easy. He said that following him meant death as well as life. Death to the old way of living, then accepting new life, new power, new standards from the Lord. All this is very tough. Many people disguise their cowardice by adopting other attitudes, such as indifference: "I'm not the religious kind." But cowardice it remains. The Man of Nazareth is too demanding, too uncompromising, too loving, too upright for the soft and compromising, the lazy and those who like to go with the crowd.

The matter of fulfillment

Another question I would like to ask the person who is not interested in religion: *do you want to find fulfillment?* Jesus once described the kingdom of God as finding treasure. Imagine a farmer plowing his field, drearily, monotonously, without any special expectations. Then his plowshare hits a box. He investigates and finds to his amazement that the box is full of diamonds and rubies. Whose heart would not beat faster at such a discovery? That, Jesus implied, is what discovering God's kingdom is like. For the kingdom is brought to us in the person of the King; and the King is Jesus. Really, then, Christianity has nothing to do with "religion" and its demands and observances.

The Christian life is concerned with relationships. First comes the restoration of our relationship with God, then the restoration of our links with others, as the basic harmony brought by Christ spreads outward. Relationships are among the most precious things in life. Yet too often they are spoiled by selfishness, racial prejudice, jealousy, or pride. Jesus Christ unites people and brings harmony where once there was discord, and that spells fulfillment at the deepest level of all.

I think of a painfully shy student who found a living faith in Christ during his first weekend at the university. Within six weeks he had opened up like a flower and was relating with far greater freedom to others. I think of a couple whose marriage was on the point of breaking up when both partners were brought to faith in Jesus. Their new relationship with Christ brought them closer together than ever before, and their marriage is now strong and happy. I think of a soldier, loathed for his conceitedness and rudeness, whose whole attitude to others changed radically when he allowed Jesus Christ to take control of him. I think of two schoolboys who could not stand each other until both of them found Christ over the same summer vacation; thereafter relationships were on a completely new plane (I should know, for I was one of the boys). This same Jesus draws together those whom every pressure in the world is driving apart. He does it in Northern Ireland, as genuine believers (as opposed to the "religious kind," be they Protestant or Catholic) have for years met across the border at night to pray for one another, support each other's widows, and tend each other's wounded. He does it in the Middle East as he brings together in one fellowship of true believers the political irreconcilables—Jews and Arabs. He does it in South Africa, between believers of different races. Time and time again I have seen all three of the above situations with my own eyes. But I know no other force on earth that can do the same. Jesus is treasure indeed, for he brings fulfillment to all our relationships, once we allow him to repair our relationship with God.

The matter of destiny

There is one other question I would like to ask the person who is not interested in religion: *are you interested in your future?* Who is not? Our education, our aspirations, our longing to succeed, our hunger for promotion are all geared to this end—securing a better future. But what happens after we've obtained our heart's desires? Is there not an emptiness at the top? Money does not satisfy permanently, nor does sex, nor does fame, nor does manipulating others. And many of the people at the top know it. The actress Raquel Welch has been quoted as saying:

> I had acquired everything I wanted, yet I was totally miserable
> ... I thought it was very peculiar that I had acquired everything I
> had wanted as a child—wealth, fame and accomplishment in my
> career. I had beautiful children, and a life style that seemed
> terrific, yet I was totally and miserably unhappy. I found it very
> frightening that one could acquire all these things and still be so
> miserable.

After all, what is life about? Are we bound for extinction, or is there some life beyond the grave? If you are really concerned about your future, you can scarcely avoid considering the matter of final destiny. Pascal put it at its most entertaining when he suggested that the afterlife is like a wager: if you believe in God, you are at no disadvantage in this life, and at considerable advantage in the next. If you do not believe, but find in the next that there was a next, you are most unfortunate! But to be more serious, what sense is there in shutting your eyes to the one person whom others testify as having broken the grip of death and having come back to tell us not only that there is an afterlife but how to get there? In business or in trade it would be accounted sheer folly to go for short-term gains and neglect capital appreciation—or depreciation. Yet that is just what people do who take no thought for life after death. They go for short-term goals, and prefer not to notice the fact that their capital, their life, is depreciating toward zero, when it could, if rightly invested, appreciate indefinitely. Christians assert, not just on the basis of documents written two thousand years ago but on the basis of continuing worldwide experience, that Jesus of Nazareth has broken the ultimate barrier in our universe, death. They may be right; they may not. That is what you must decide after investigation. But to shrug off the whole issue with, "I'm not the religious kind," is sheer folly, if you think at all seriously about your future.

Faith has two sides

Sometimes people say, "I'm not the religious kind," with a touch of wistfulness, similar to the way they say, "I wish I had your faith." My answer to that is simple. You can have my faith. Faith is nothing other than trust; and trust, to be any good, must have two sides to it. First, there needs to be good evidence of trustworthiness; then there needs to be genuine commitment. It is as simple as that. You have faith in Rolls-Royce engines when you fly in a jet, don't you? That means that in your opinion Rolls-Royce engines are reliable; it also means that you are prepared to entrust yourself to their trustworthiness. So it is with Christianity. You need first to be convinced that there is a God, that he cares about us, that he has revealed himself in Jesus Christ, and that it is possible for you to get in touch with him. Then you need to entrust yourself to his trustworthiness.

In the pages that follow, we shall be considering the various topics in a progression that will, I hope, help you to appreciate the trustworthiness of God and also encourage you to entrust yourself to him. Then you will have my faith. Then you will be able to say, "I'm not the religious kind, but I think I may have discovered the key to the universe."

3

"You can't believe in God these days."

God is out of fashion

Despite the opinion polls, which show that the majority of people in Western countries (not to mention the overwhelming majority in the East) do believe in God, it is amazing how often you hear the question of the Almighty dismissed in the single sentence, "Oh, you can't believe in God these days."

Very understandable, in a way. We live in a very busy age, and many of us have neither the time nor the inclination to inquire into abstruse subjects that do not directly concern us. But what if there is a God who made us, loves us, and will judge us? Well, if that is the case, as Dr. Jowett, famous head of an Oxford college, once put it, "It is not what I think of God, but what God thinks of me that matters."

Again, the idea of God has been so abused in the past that we tend to shy away from it. God has been portrayed as the man in the sky with the big stick. We have been told to be good and to do the right thing because God will judge us if we do the wrong thing. God's will has been found to be a very useful tool for keeping people in their places:

> The rich man in his castle,
> The poor man at his gate;
> God made them high and lowly,
> And ordered their estate.

A whole system of social and racial oppression has been founded on that view of God, expressed here in a verse—which is now always omitted!—from the hymn "All Things Bright and Beautiful." Indeed, God's will is something that certain people in certain ages have claimed to be so sure about that they have engaged in religious wars, like the Crusades, or religious persecutions, like the Inquisition, to press their point. God has, furthermore, been used as a sort of plug to fill in the gaps of scientific knowledge; even Sir Isaac Newton postulated God to keep the universe and its laws going. But as scientific knowledge has grown, the gaps have shrunk, and God with them.

For all these reasons God is out of fashion. As *Time* magazine headlined on its cover some years back: GOD IS DEAD! But it is difficult to be sure about these things. Perhaps there is as much fashion as there is reason about it all. Just four years later the headlines of *Time* were asking: IS GOD COMING TO LIFE AGAIN? After all, you get no justification for religious wars or inquisitions in the Bible. You do not find this handbook of Christianity maintaining that you should do good in case God should punish you for your failures. Nowhere in the Bible is God used to plug in the gaps of human knowledge; instead, he is portrayed as the source and sustainer and goal of the whole universe, including man and his knowledge. Perhaps we ought to look a little more closely at the claim that you can't believe, these days. What is so special about these days that makes it harder for us to believe in God than it was for our fathers?

The problem of suffering
Many find the problem of suffering a major obstacle to believing in God. Not that the amount of suffering is greater than ever before, but it seems greater. It is brought into the living room every night on TV. How can there be a God if he allows all this pain and anguish in his world?

I do not want to minimize this problem for one moment. It is by far the strongest argument against the existence of God.

But suppose, for a minute, that the problem of pain drives you to reject God's existence and to imagine that either some monster rules our destinies or that the stars are in charge of our fortunes; how does that help? You may have gotten rid of the problems of evil and pain (though you still have to live with them) but you have replaced them with a much bigger problem: how do you get kindness and humanity, love and unselfishness, gentleness and goodness in a world that is governed by a horrid monster or uncaring stars? No, that way does not help.

As a matter of fact, the Christian has a greater insight into the insoluble problem of suffering (and it remains insoluble, whatever philosophy of life you adopt) than anyone else. For the Scriptures teach us that God is no stranger to pain. He did not create the world and then leave it callously to its own devices. He does not willingly afflict us and take delight in torturing us. The very reverse. He cares so much about the agony and pain of this struggling world of his that he got involved in it personally. He came as a man among men. He lived in squalor and suffering; he knew thirst and hunger, flogging and heartbreak, fear and despair. His life ended in one of the most excruciating ways known to humanity. Let nobody tell me that God doesn't care! Let nobody claim that the boss doesn't know what life is like on the factory floor!

Take a long hard look at the cross. Through that cross God is telling you that he does care about pain. He cares passionately and selflessly. He cares so much that he came to share it. He is forever the suffering God. The cross tells me that God loves me even in the midst of pain and suffering; when everything looked its bleakest, Jesus was still the supreme object of his heavenly Father's love. Moreover, through that cross I can vaguely discern another truth: that God uses pain. He turns evil into good. For it was evil, real evil, that crucified Jesus. And yet, by the way he took it, he overcame evil. He turned hatred to love in some, at least, of his persecutors. He gave an example of innocent, uncomplaining suffering that has inspired people ever since, and enabled men like Bishop Wilson [1] to forgive and win the hearts of some of those who tortured him in a Japanese prison camp in the Second World War, by means of his courage and spirit. And what makes such triumph over pain possible? Not merely the example of the cross of Jesus. One needs more than an example in the midst of agony. There was something else about the cross that has rubbed off on Christians ever since. It is the sense of victory. On the first Good Friday, Jesus died with a cry of triumph on his lips: triumph over pain, hatred, suffering, and death. And that was not the end. He rose from the chilly grip of the tomb on the third day. From that moment on, he enjoys the power of an endless life.

Christians are people who have put their trust in him, have come to know him, and have begun to taste the power of his risen and endless life. How is it that the early Christians could look cheerfully at death in the arena from wild beasts and gladiators, or being roasted on a grid? Simply because they were convinced that evil and pain had suffered utter defeat through what God had done on that cross of Calvary and the resulting resurrection. Even death was a defeated foe. So they came to look at suffering not as an unmitigated evil but as an evil that had been conquered by their suffering and triumphant God; an evil that he could even use to discipline them, to refine them, and to equip them for further usefulness and deeper Christlikeness. And the suffering but victorious God, the sinless but sin-bearing God, has given on the cross of Christ a trailer of his future film. Christians could safely trust him to shed more light on it all in the life to come, knowing that there would be a further explanation of the mystery of the cross, where, in the very midst of history, God showed that he cared about pain, shared it, and overcame it. To be sure, the Christian need not

---

1. Bishop Leonard Wilson was the Anglican Bishop of Singapore during its occupation by the Japanese.

be worried that suffering in the world makes belief in God impossible these days. It is only belief in a suffering God that stops us from either becoming totally callous or going out of our minds at all the suffering that afflicts our world.

The problem of meaninglessness

Second, there's the problem of meaninglessness. Never before in human history has there been such a widespread belief that in the end nothing matters; we came from nothing, and we go to nothing. No values are implanted in us, because there is no God to implant them; no part of the human frame survives death, because there is no eternity. Meaning has disappeared from life. More money, more leisure, yes; but don't talk to us about meaning in life, because there isn't any. A leading modern painter, Francis Bacon, writes:

> Man now realizes that he is an accident, that he is a completely futile being, that he has to play out the game without reason. Earlier artists were still conditioned by certain types of religious possibilities, which man now, you could say, has had cancelled out for him. Man can now only attempt to beguile himself for a time by prolonging his life—by buying a kind of immortality through the doctors. . . . The artist must really deepen the game to be any good at all, so that he can make life a bit more exciting.[2]

What the artist has done is to bring home this meaninglessness to every level of society. It comes through films and pop music. It is everywhere. Dirk Bogarde said, as his career took off, "I rather liked it all. There was one wavering doubt, however, just one. Who the hell was I? There was a vast vacuum, and in spite of a house, car, all my family and possessions, I belonged nowhere."[3] Nobel Prize winner Jacques Monod proclaimed,

2. Michael Peppiatt, *Francis Bacon: Anatomy of an Enigma* (Weidenfeld & Nicholson, 1997).
3. John Coldstream, *Dirk Bogarde: The Authorized Biography* (Weidenfeld & Nicholson, 2004).

"The universe was not pregnant with life, nor the biosphere with meaning. Our number came up in the Monte Carlo game."[4] It reminds me of words on a French gravestone: "Here lies a man who went out of the world without knowing why he came into it."

Now if you are eaten up with this philosophy of meaninglessness, of course you won't find any sense in God talk. But it is a chicken and egg situation. The philosophy of meaninglessness is an attempt by modern existentialists to draw the full consequences from atheism. Deny God, and then see if you can make sense of everything else. And the fact is that you can't.

But try it the other way around. What if there is a God? Then the world is not merely a fluke; it is the result of his creation. Humanity is not rubbish but God's deputy on this earth. History is not bunk but God's story struggling for expression through all the follies of humankind. Life is not meant to be understood simply in terms of the threescore years and ten but as a training ground for being with God forever. No longer need we be torn between the very obvious order and purpose in nature and the purposelessness, meaninglessness, and lostness that modern human beings find in their hearts. If only we will return to the Creator of order and purpose in nature, we will begin to find order coming through in our own lives, and a sense of purpose in cooperating with the Creator in the management of his world.

The problem of proof

The third problem is the matter of proof. "You can't prove God," they say. That's true. You can't. But you can't prove that your mother loves you, either. In fact, there are precious few things that you can prove, and they are by no means the most

4. Connie Barlow, ed., quoted in *Evolution Extended* (MIT Press, 1994), 180–98.

interesting things in life. To prove a thing really means to show that it could not be otherwise, a very final form of certainty. You cannot prove that the sun will rise tomorrow. You cannot prove that you are alive. You cannot prove the link between cause and effect that runs through every action we perform. You cannot prove that you are the same person you were ten years ago. The philosopher David Hume attempted to prove the link between cause and effect and between himself as he then was and himself ten years previously, and he failed. Failed utterly. Proof is only applicable to very rarefied areas of philosophy and mathematics, and even here there is debate. For the most part, we are driven to acting on good evidence, without the luxury of proof. There is good evidence of the link between cause and effect. There is good reason to believe that I am the same man as I was ten years ago. There is good reason to suppose that my mother really loves me and is not just fattening me up for the moment when she will put arsenic in my tea. And there is good reason to believe in God. Very good reason. Not conclusive proof but very good reason, just the same. Let me outline to you why I believe it is much harder to reject the existence of a supreme being than to accept it.

1. The fact of our world

Look at the fact of our world. As far as we know at present, this planet is the only part of the universe where there is life. What accounts for this world of ours? Whether we go for the big bang theory or the steady state theory, we are driven to ask *why* it should be so. The world must have come from somewhere. It's not enough to reply, "It is just one of those things." It's not enough to assign the whole thing to chance. If the world is attributable to chance, how is it that cause and effect are built into that world at every turn? It isn't very rational to suppose that chance gives birth to cause and effect! And it isn't very rational to suppose that a world based on cause and effect is itself uncaused. Aldous Huxley once said, "The link between cause and effect is the chief article in the scientist's creed."[5] If you think hard enough, science itself drives you back to believe in a Creator.

2. The fact of design

Look at the fact of design. At every level, the world of nature shows evidence of design. Think of the focusing equipment of an eye, of the radar of a bat, of the built-in gyroscope of a swallow, of the camouflage of a nesting pheasant. Or think of the perfect harmony of the laws of physics. Reflect on the marvel of conception and birth. At every point there is evidence of a great Designer. Even John Stuart Mill, a strong opponent of Christianity, came to the conclusion at the end of his life that, "The argument from design is irresistible. Nature does testify to its Creator."[6] Albert Einstein, too, spoke of his "humble admiration for the illimitable superior Spirit who reveals himself in the slight details which we can perceive with our frail mind."[7] After Einstein had propounded his theory of relativity, and after its general acceptance following the Michelson–Morley experiment, the experiment was repeated and provided different results. But nobody doubted the relativity theory! Everyone assumed (rightly as it turned out) that the results must be due to experimental error, because the theory was too good, *too rational,* to be false. In other words, the physicists themselves were operating on the assumption of design in the universe, however much they might have claimed to be following merely experimental results.

Okay then, if there is design in the world, where did it come from? Not from us; we don't lay down the laws of nature or design the development of the fetus in the womb. It looks very much as though a Designer is at work.

5. Aldous Huxley et al., *Complete Essays of Aldous Huxley*, vol. 1 (Ivan R. Dee Inc., 2000).
6. John Stuart Mill, *Three Essays on Religion* (Greenwood Press), 1974.
7. James B. Simpson, *Simpson's Contemporary Quotations* (HarperCollins, 1996).

Modern physics has gone a long way toward reinforcing this suspicion with the *anthropic principle*. This principle suggests that the world looks very much as though it has been designed for human beings to live in it. If things were only slightly different, life would be impossible. If gravity was stronger, we would not be able to move. If it was weaker, we would fly off the ground!

Professor John Polkinghorne, himself a brilliant physicist, writes in *The Way the World Is* of the

> increasing realization that there is a delicate and intricate balance in the structure of the world for the emergence of life. Suppose things had been a little different in those crucial first three minutes when the gross nuclear structure of the world got fixed as a quarter helium and three-quarters hydrogen. If things had gone a little faster, all would have been helium; and without hydrogen how could water (vital to life) have been able to form?

He concludes,

> Scientists are aware of a number of critical considerations of this type which, taken together, produce a fairly tight-knit series of constraints on the way the world must be in order that we are here to observe it. They call the collection of these constraints the anthropic principle.[8]

They do indeed. And it provides a powerful demonstration of the design that runs through the universe.

The argument of the design aspect is extremely persuasive, and to say with Jean-Paul Sartre, "This world is not the product of Intelligence. It meets our gaze as would a crumpled piece of paper.... What is man but a little puddle of water whose freedom is death?"[9] is to shut your eyes to one of the clearest indications that there is a Creator God who has not left himself without witness. "The heavens are telling the glory of God; and

8. John Polkinghorne, *The Way the World Is* (Eerdmans, 1984).
9. Jean-Paul Sartre, *Existentialism and Humanism* (Methuen, 1974).

the firmament proclaims his handiwork" (Ps. 19:1) remains true: so does the Bible's assertion, "The fool says in his heart, 'There is no God'" (Ps. 14:1).

3. The fact of personality

Look at the fact of personality. It is one of the most remarkable phenomena in the world. The difference between a person and a thing, between a live person and a dead one, is fundamental. When Sartre, in the quotation given above, denied that the world was created by Intelligence, he was insulting not only his Maker but also his own power of reasoning. He was saying, in effect, that there was no reason to believe what he was saying! The fact is that we are not mere robots; there is more to us than that, namely, human personality. Some thinkers are so reluctant to believe this that they have advanced the improbable creed of materialism, seeking to reduce everything in life to what can be measured scientifically. In other words, other people are mere blobs of protoplasm; so am I. I think I am a conscious, rational being who can mix with others like me. But no. Materialism knows nothing of rationality and consciousness, of personality and sociability. It deals only with molecules and magnetism, elements and electricity, things that can be counted and measured. I have no place in such language, and if that is the ultimate language of reality, then I cannot describe myself and am driven to the conclusion that I do not exist. Not very plausible. But the alternative is disturbing. It suggests that my personality cannot be explained simply in terms of its physical components. I am more than matter. But how can I be, if there is no God? Does a river run higher than its source? Of course not. Then how do we get human personality out of the inorganic matter that is the brute stuff of which our universe is entirely composed, in the atheist view? Can rationality and life spring from chance and nonbeing? No, the fact of human personality is another impressive pointer to the God who created us in his own image. This is not to say that God is restricted to a personality like ours, but it is to say that the ultimate source of our being is not less than personal.

4. The fact of values

Look at the fact of values. We all have them, but they are very hard to understand if there is no God. After all, you don't expect to find values knocking around in molecules! Matter does not give rise to morals. So modern godless people are confused about where our values fit in. We value life—but why should we, if life really springs from chance? We value truth—but why should we, if there is no ultimate reality? We value goodness—but what is that doing in a world derived from plankton? We revel in beauty—but there is nothing in it, since it too springs from the chaos in which our world originated. We value communication—but the universe is silent. Yes, we have our values, and they do not mesh very well with the atheist's picture of the world, sprung merely from chance, matter, and millions of years to allow for extensive development. I do not find much basis for value judgments there.

But what if there is a Creator God? Then life is valuable because it is his greatest gift, hence the infinite value of every individual. Truth matters because it is one aspect of God, the ultimate reality. Beauty and goodness are likewise two of the "faces" of God, and every good action or beautiful sight is an inkling of the good and beautiful source from which they come. Best of all, we do not inhabit a silent planet: God has spoken and revealed himself, to some extent at least, in the world, in its design, in values, and in human beings. When we communicate, it is not vain jabbering but a God-given ability, entrusted to us by the great Communicator himself. Those are two basic attitudes to values. I know which one makes more sense to me. John Lucas, the Oxford philosopher, develops this argument clearly and simply: "I want to do well. But it is impossible to do well unless there are values independent of me by which my performance can be assessed. I cannot want to do only what I want to do, or I am denying my nature as a rational agent."[10] The existence of values is a pointer to God that is very difficult to evade.

5. The fact of conscience

Look at the fact of conscience. That's a pointer to God if ever there was one. Your conscience doesn't argue. It acts like a lawgiver inside you, acquitting you or condemning you. It doesn't say, "Do this because you will gain by it," or "Do it because you will escape trouble that way." It just says, "Do it." It is a most remarkable pointer to the God who put it there. Oh, of course it is not the voice of God, straight and simple. It has been warped by all sorts of things: our environment, our rationalizations, our disobedience. But, equally certain, conscience can't just be explained away as the pressure of society. It was not from any pressure of society that John Newton and William Wilberforce conscientiously fought for the liberation of slaves, or Martin Luther King championed the cause of black people. Their actions were carried out in the teeth of opposition by society, and so it has always been with every moral advance.

Despite the diversity of human cultures the world over, there is actually remarkable agreement on the essential values to which conscience points: the general condemnation of murder and theft, of adultery and lust, of hijacking and torture. There is universal agreement that peace is right and war is wrong; that love is right and hate is wrong—however seldom human beings manage to carry it out in practice. And it is conscience that points us to this difference between right and wrong, and the claim that right has upon us. C. S. Lewis summed it up like this: "If no set of moral ideas were better than another, there would be no sense in preferring civilized morality to Nazi morality.

10. John Randolph Lucas, *The Freedom of the Will* (Oxford University Press, 1970).

The moment you say one lot of morals is better than another, you are in fact measuring them by an ultimate standard."[11] Even the thinker Bertrand Russell, who during the earlier part of his life fought tooth and nail against the idea of an ultimate distinction between right and wrong, said, toward the end of his life, "To love is right, to hate is wrong."[12] But how does he get such moral absolutes in what he claimed is a godless world? It doesn't add up. You cannot locate principles of conscience in a chance collection of atoms, which is all the world consists of, if you remove the possibility of a Creator. No—morality, conscience, the difference between right and wrong are important indicators of a God who is interested in what is right and good and true. He is no blind force, no abstruse designer, but a personal God, so concerned with what is right that he has built a moral indicator into each one of his creatures.

6. The fact of religion

Look at the fact of religion. We are religious animals. In the sixth century BC, philosophers in Greece poured scorn on religion and told people to grow up. Religion continued. And so it has done everywhere in the world ever since. The Russians sought to abolish religion after the revolution in 1917. They failed. They tried again with violent persecution under Stalin. They failed. And now the gospel has free rein in Russia! People are incurably religious. We are going to worship either God or a pseudogod, but worship something we will, even if it is something very physical, like our material prosperity, or something very abstract, like the idea of progress.

> There is one fact about man that has distinguished him since his first appearance on earth. It marks him as different from all other creatures. That is, he's a worshipping animal. Wherever he has existed there are the remains, in some form or other, of his

11. C. S. Lewis, *Mere Christianity* (HarperCollins, 2001).
12. Bertrand Russell, *The Autobiography* (Routledge, 2000).

worship. That's not a pious conclusion: it's an observed fact. And all through history and prehistory when he's deprived himself of that, he's gone to pieces. Many people nowadays are going to pieces, or they find the first convenient prop to tie their instincts on to. It's behind the extraordinary adulation of royalty. It's behind the mobbing of TV stars. If you don't give expression to an instinct you've got to sublimate it or go out of your mind.[13]

Such is the conclusion not of a philosopher or priest but of a novelist, Winston Graham, in *The Sleeping Partner*. He's right, isn't he?

These are some of the facts that, taken together, not only make belief in God reasonable but also make it very hard to rationally deny his existence. They point to a God who is skillful, skillful enough to design the paths of the stars and the development of a fetus. They point to a God who is the source of human personality and therefore not less than personal, however much he may transcend all that we mean by that word. He is the ultimate source of our values; life, language, truth, beauty, and goodness find their ultimate home in him. He is so concerned about right and wrong that he has furnished each of his creatures with a conscience. And he wants us to know him and to enjoy him, to worship and live in his company—hence the universal religious instinct of men and women through history and all over the world.

13. Winston Graham, *The Sleeping Partner* (Fontana, 1997).

4

"Science has defeated faith!"

Sir Richard Gregory, sometime editor of *Nature*, was one of those unusual people who wrote his own epitaph. It ran like this:

> My grandfather preached the gospel of Christ
> My father preached the gospel of socialism
> I preach the gospel of science.[14]

That attitude is increasingly common. When my father was a boy, there were no cars, no airplanes, and most people never moved more than a few miles from their own village. The change to highways, space travel, nuclear fission, and the Internet—not to mention the global village—all happened in his lifetime. The astonishing advances in medicine, interstellar travel, and subatomic physics induce such a feeling of confidence in our human potential that the idea of God seems strangely dated. It is hardly surprising that Christians are ridiculed for their old-fashioned, unscientific ideas. With their talk of God and Satan, of heaven and hell, of salvation and loss, they are not only hopelessly off target, not only burbling complete irrelevancies, but they are simply deluding themselves. The man in the street reckons that science has killed off religion. A good deal of what he sees on television confirms his suspicions, and a glance at the exterior of the church round the corner, with its shabby bulletin board, its advertised activities,

14. W. H. G. Armytage, *Sir Richard Gregory: His Life and Work* (Macmillan, 1956).

and the people who go there makes it clear to him that between science and religion there is a yawning gulf. The former is modern and useful; the latter, old-fashioned and useless. The former works and the latter manifestly does not. Richard Dawkins, the Oxford zoologist, is militant on the subject. "What has theology ever said that is of the smallest use to anybody? What has theology ever said that is demonstrably true and is not obvious?"[15] The man in the street may not be as harsh as that, but who can blame him for ditching the idea of God?

Christian origins of science

That would all seem very odd to the scientific pioneers of the sixteenth and seventeenth centuries. For the truly remarkable thing about the growth of modern science is that it took place in a Christian civilization, recently liberated from the shackles of authoritarianism by the Renaissance and the Reformation. What's more, it was pioneered by committed Christians. Francis Bacon saw God's works in nature and his words in the Bible as twin facets of his self-disclosure. So did Johannes Kepler, who revolutionized the astronomical prejudice of his day, derived from Plato, that there are only circular movements among the heavenly bodies. When he did his scientific study, he felt himself to be "thinking God's thoughts after him." He was, he felt, "a high priest in the book of nature, religiously bound not to alter one jot or tittle of what it had pleased God to write down in it."[16] That is why he took very seriously the eight degrees of divergence from the circular in Mars's orbit,

15. Richard Dawkins, in an article entitled "The Emptiness of Theology," originally published in *Free Inquiry Magazine*, Council for Secular Humanism, Amherst, NY, vol. 18, no. 2, and online at http://www.positiveatheism.org/writ/dawkins2.htm#EMPTY. For a detailed repudiation of Dawkins' atheism, see A. E. McGrath, *Dawkins' God* (Blackwell, 2005).
16. Job Kozhamthadam, *The Discovery of Kepler's Laws: The Interaction of Science, Philosophy and Religion* (University of Notre Dame Press, 1993).

which he discovered by observation and thereby paved the way for the reformation of astronomy.

Galileo and Copernicus remained Christians, convinced that their work glorified God, despite the provocation afforded them due to the opposition toward the spread of knowledge by the Roman Catholic Church of the day. Sir Isaac Newton wrote his *Principia* in the assurance that "this world could originate from nothing but the perfectly free will of God."[17] He is said to have spent more time in biblical study than in scientific research.

Robert Boyle, one of the founders of the Royal Society,[18] was a sincere Christian, and he gave a lecture for "proving the Christian religion against notorious infidels."[19] Many of the other founders of the Royal Society shared Boyle's faith, men like Seth Ward, John Wallis, Bishop John Wilkins, and Isaac Barrow. They saw no contradiction in directing their studies equally "to the glory of God" and to "the advantage of the human race." They would assuredly have seen nothing incongruous in the inscription over the gateway of the Cavendish Laboratory in Cambridge: "The works of the Lord are great, sought out by all those who have pleasure therein." Science was clearly not seen as the enemy of Christianity in those days.

Science, atheism, and belief

It would be a great mistake to think that scientists were believers in the early days, whereas today they are an agnostic bunch. As a recent survey shows, among top scientists at present some 40 percent are believers, the same proportion unbelievers, and 20 percent are not convinced one way or the other. There have always been both atheists and Christians

17. Sir Isaac Newton, *The Principia: Mathematical Principles of Natural Philosophy* (University of California Press, 1999).
18. The independent scientific academy of the UK dedicated to promoting excellence in science.
19. M. A. Stewart, *Robert Boyle Selected Papers* (Hackett Publishing, 1991).

in the ranks of the scientists, as in other disciplines. There were many children of the Enlightenment in the seventeenth and eighteenth centuries who combined their empirical approach to reality with disdain of God. Men like David Hume, Herbert Spencer, and John Stuart Mill were among the architects of today's atheistic humanism.

So when the Russian authorities decreed after the revolution that the last vestiges of religious faith must be wiped out by scientific propaganda, on the assumption that religion will disappear once the true light of science dawns on human minds, they were not doing anything new. Bishop Joseph Butler, in the eighteenth century, had complained in his *Analogy of Religion* that,

> It is come, I know not how, to be taken for granted by many persons that Christianity is not so much as a subject for enquiry, but that it is now at length discovered to be fictitious. Accordingly they treated it as if in this present age, this were an agreed point among all people of discernment, and nothing remained but to set it up as a principal subject of mirth and ridicule, as it were by way of reprisals for its having so long interrupted the pleasures of the world.[20]

It is an interesting reflection that, within a few years of Butler writing those words in 1736, a massive religious revival began to sweep through England through the preaching of John Wesley and George Whitefield. The whole country was profoundly affected within a generation. And in 1989 the Berlin Wall fell, Eastern Europe was set free from Communist domination, and a religious revival set in. The same is true in China despite the official continuation of Communism. And in the face of much sociological prediction that religion would be a dead issue by the year 2000 or thereabouts, we have seen in the twentieth century a massive resurgence of dynamic Christianity, not least in the shape of half a billion Pentecostal

20. Joseph Butler, *The Analogy of Religion* (Classworks, 1986).

Christians, who simply did not exist before the year 1900! And
as we survey the resurgence of Islam, to mention but one major
faith, it is apparent that, so far from lying down and dying in
this age of advanced scientific knowledge, religion has become
the most significant political and social issue in the world.

Then why the apparent opposition?

Battle was joined in the nineteenth century. The work of
three distinguished Victorians, Sigmund Freud, Karl Marx,
and Charles Darwin, combined to change the attitude of the
country toward God. Religion came to be seen in educated
circles as illusory, the product of human beings seeking
consolation—a situation that would evaporate with the escala-
tion of scientific advance.

Freud certainly saw religion as illusory, arising from the
human unconscious. He believed that when Christians talk
about God as their heavenly Father, they are projecting into
the empty skies a projection of their own father. He claimed
that through psychoanalysis he had found an answer to this
universal neurosis. But his atheism did not come as a result of
his studies; he was an atheist before he started. In fact, he
became a psychoanalyst precisely because he was an atheist
and felt the need to explain why anyone would be so stupid as
to believe in God. Had he not heard of the danger of circular
arguments? But his position is subject to other serious criti-
cisms and no longer holds the field in psychoanalytic studies.

Thus he failed to distinguish between religious fantasy of the
mentally ill, with whom he was largely occupied profession-
ally, and the very large number of healthy and intelligent
people who believed in God. Again, he was forced to justify his
assumption that Christianity was an amalgam of fantasy and
emotionalism by the desperate expedient that we could know
nothing of the historical Jesus! A further difficulty in his
position is the boomerang nature of the argument. He writes

off Christianity as wish fulfillment and obsessional neurosis but seems unaware that the same arguments could be applied to his own pansexual theory of psychoanalysis. How about "the beginnings of art, religion, ethics, and society all meet in the Oedipus complex" as a bit of obsessional nonsense? Yes, this was Freud's fantastic claim in *Totem and Tabu*. Those who write off what they do not understand as illusory must not be surprised at the retort of *tu quoque* (you too).

Karl Marx was a materialist: the world consists only of matter without any spiritual dimensions. He believed that every aspect of life is determined by social and political factors. And the idea of God is merely a human attempt to cope with the harshness of life as he had observed it on the continent and in his own miserable exile. Human beings make religion. In particular, those in power find it useful for keeping the masses down. It is only the product of social and economic alienation. Once change the social and political scene, and people will forget the illusory comfort of religion and embrace the joys of improved living conditions. Social revolution would be the great liberator of downtrodden humanity. As soon as Communism is in place, religion will fade away.

Such was the theory. But it did not turn out like that, did it? When Communism was introduced into Russia in 1917, it came with blood and sword, and so it continued. Far from being a liberator, it slaughtered millions and crushed the human spirit. The people who stood out against it at enormous personal cost were the Christians and their friends, men like author Aleksandr Solzhenitsyn. Marxism stands discredited. That experiment of wholehearted atheism failed comprehensively in Russia and Eastern Europe, and it is failing in Cuba and China, the only two places in the globe where it is being retained.

The third great Victorian who paved the way for unbelief in the name of science was Charles Darwin. He was considering ordination as a young man, but his scientific studies drew him in a very different direction. It is fashionable to think of Darwin as a complete atheist. This is far from the case. His views about God were confused and uncoordinated. It would be fair to say that he moved more in an unbelieving direction as he grew older, and for two main reasons. First, the death of his much-loved daughter and, second, the doctrine of conscious unending torment in hell that was much in favor among Victorian preachers. Not surprisingly, his soul reacted strongly against it. It was not his theory of natural selection that drove him away from God. The two can be perfectly compatible.

Asa Grey, the distinguished American Darwinian, held strongly to the theory of evolution and equally as strongly to a committed Christian worldview. After all, God may be behind the evolutionary process. He may equally have bestowed autonomy upon creation and allowed the world to make itself from the bottom up, so to speak. Charles Kingsley argued that "it is just as noble a conception of Deity to believe that he had created primal forms capable of self-development as to believe that he required a fresh act of intervention to supply the lacunas he himself had made."[21] I can't argue with that. Can you?

Conclusion

Let us be very clear about the matter of the theory of evolution, because so many people come unglued over it. The theory of evolution (and it is only a theory) sets out to explain how varied forms of life have developed from more simple forms over millions of years. Belief in a Creator sets out to explain that there is a great mind behind all matter. There is no necessary contradiction between the two. Stephen Jay Gould, who died in 2002, was one of the world's greatest experts on evolutionary theory. He is forthright on the subject:

21. Written in a letter from Kingsley to Charles Darwin recorded in *The Life and Letters of Charles Darwin*, vol. 2, by Francis Darwin (Indypublish.com, 2002).

To say it for the umpteenth million [time,] ... science simply cannot adjudicate the issue of God's possible superintendence of nature. We neither affirm nor deny it. We simply can't comment on it as scientists. If some of our crowd have made untoward statements claiming that Darwinism disproves God then I will find Mrs. McInerney [his old schoolmistress!] and have their knuckles rapped for it (as long as she can equally treat those members of our crowd who have argued that Darwinism must be God's method of action).

His conclusion? "Either half my colleagues are enormously stupid, or else the science of Darwinism is fully compatible with conventional religious beliefs—and equally compatible with atheism."[22]

There is nothing in the scientific method that can either demonstrate God's existence or disprove it. But for what it is worth, the basic presupposition of the scientific method strongly supports the existence of mind behind matter. It is axiomatic for all scientific inquiries that there is order and purpose in the physical world. Why should this be if the world sprang from chaos? There are very few pure materialists around these days, for it is abundantly obvious that analysis of physical laws and chemical constituents cannot explain human behavior, let alone reason, emotion, wonder, speech, morals, and worship. "There are more things in heaven and earth than are dreamed of in your philosophy."[23] These words of Shakespeare are applicable to the person who tries to make scientific materialism the only arbiter of truth. There is nothing in scientific procedure, still less in the theory of evolution, that need embarrass any believer in God the Creator.

22. Stephen Jay Gould, *Rocks of Ages: Science and Religion in the Fullness of Life* (Ballantine, 1999).
23. William Shakespeare, *Hamlet* (I, v, 166–167).

5

"Didn't Jesus have a baby with Mary Magdalene?"

This question might seem bizarre, but I would be surprised if you have not had it raised in conversation or on television. Such ideas have come to the fore with two popular books that have had soaring sales. The first was *Holy Blood, Holy Grail*, written by Michael Baigent, Richard Leigh, and Henry Lincoln in the 1980s. Its fortunes have been revived through the second book, which takes much the same line. It is *The Da Vinci Code*, written by Dan Brown and published in 2003. It has remained at or near the top of the *New York Times* best-seller list for over a year as I write, and is somewhat less celebrated in Britain but still wildly popular. It has seven million hardback copies in circulation and apparently has already been translated into more than forty languages. A film version of the book will emerge in 2005.

Although the books, the films, and the TV programs may be here today and gone tomorrow, the topic is worth looking at because it calls into question the reliability of the New Testament picture of Jesus and offers us a very different one. For the sake of simplicity, I shall confine my examination to the version of Jesus in *The Da Vinci Code*.

First, let me say what an enthralling read this six-hundred-page blockbuster is. It is fast moving, gripping, intelligent, and fun. The reviews run out of superlatives. "More satisfying twists than a licorice factory" is the verdict of *Booklist.* "A whopper of a plot that will please conspiracy buffs and thriller addicts alike," claims *Publishers Weekly.* "This novel takes off down a road that is as eye-opening as it is page-turning. You simply cannot put it down," writes author Vince Flynn in the *New York Times.* And so say all of them. They are right. It is a fast-moving and engrossing cliff-hanger. I greatly enjoyed it.

The main plot is roughly as follows. Jacques Saunière, curator of the Louvre and an expert on Renaissance art, is found murdered in the museum. Suspicion falls on Robert Langdon, a Harvard professor of symbology (Brown's new word) who is an expert in religious icons and the occult. He has recently completed a book entitled *Symbols of the Lost Sacred Feminine.* He and Sophie Neveu, a beautiful cryptographer and estranged granddaughter of Saunière, team up and escape the clutches of the French police. After a merry chase around the environs of Paris, their quest for the legendary Holy Grail (hinted at through certain circumstances in Saunière's death) takes them to England. They are accompanied by Sir Leigh Teabing, a sinister British royal historian with a house in France, who both accompanies and competes with them in the quest. It turns out that the mysterious grail is both the tomb of Mary Magdalene and also the bloodline (to which Sophie finds she belongs) of the union of Jesus and Mary Magdalene, which Brown asserts "kept recurring in the gospels." Precisely which Gospel is unclear! Some documents found in the Bibliothèque Nationale in Paris indicated that Jesus and Mary spawned the Merovingian royal line of the early Middle Ages. These have since been shown to be a complete hoax, but that does not trouble the novelist!

Throughout all this, there is a subplot, which is an attack on Christianity and particularly the Roman Catholic Church. The fourth-century emperor Constantine started the deception, so the book maintains. In a move to confirm his power, Constantine commissioned a new Bible that omitted and suppressed the Gnostic gospels. The Catholic Church tried to expunge this account of the Jesus and Magdalene affair and eliminate their descendants. But the Priory of Sion, a secret society opposed to the power of the Vatican, has kept the secret history of the Grail alive and celebrates it with a bizarre sex ritual called *hieros gamos,* sacred marriage—intercourse between the priory's leader and a woman to celebrate the "sacred feminine" and embody the connection between the erotic and the sacred expunged by orthodox Christianity. The package of suspense, sex, spirituality, and attacks on the church makes a powerful mix, which suits a great many tastes in an age that is doubtful of Christianity but hungry for spirituality.

Of course, this is just a novel, but Brown wants to be taken seriously in his revisionist account of Christian origins. Not only does he claim that Sir Isaac Newton, Sandro Botticelli, and Leonardo da Vinci were members of the Priory of Sion (which did not exist in their day!), but he is emphatic "that all descriptions of artwork, architecture, documents and secret rituals are accurate."[24] As we shall see, they are not. And it is not only conservative Christians who say so. Mark Burrows, a United Church of Christ historian, in his extended review of the book, observes, "Almost everything Brown asserts or implies as fact is misleading or mistaken.... Mostly the latter."[25]

This is not the place for a detailed review of the book nor a defense of the history of the church, which has often been unworthy of Christ. But because this sort of claim is likely to be made again, it is worth examining four of the main assertions in books like *The Da Vinci Code* that relate to Jesus Christ, and the evidence upon which those claims are made.

24. Dan Brown, *The Da Vinci Code* (Doubleday Books, 2003).
25. From an article by Mark Burrows, in *The Christian Century,* 4 June 2004.

Was Jesus not declared divine before the fourth century?

The book claims that belief in Jesus's divinity was not invented until the fourth century.

> "Until that moment in history Jesus was viewed by his followers as a mortal prophet ... a great and powerful man but a *man* nonetheless," pontificated Teabing.
> "Not the Son of God?" asks Sophie.
> "Right," replied Teabing. "Jesus's establishment as the Son of God was officially proposed and voted on by the Council of Nicaea ... and a relatively close vote at that."

Well, the truth of the matter is that the Council of Nicaea in AD 325 was attended by 220 bishops, and all but two of them asserted that Jesus is "of one substance with the Father." But they did so not because they were inventing it for the first time but to disassociate themselves from an influential man called Arius who could not believe that Jesus quite shared the Father's nature.

The deity of Jesus was very clearly taught in the New Testament, 250 years earlier, and had been passionately believed by the early church. For example, "in him the whole fulness of deity dwells bodily" (Col. 2:9) or "though he was in the form of God, did not count equality with God a thing to be grasped, but emptied himself, taking the form of a servant, being born in the likeness of men" (Phil. 2:6–7). There are many such references in the Epistles written in the fifties and sixties of the first century. Here is one from the dignified beginning of the letter to the Hebrews:

> He [God] has spoken to us by his Son, whom he appointed heir of all things, and through whom he made the universe. The Son is the radiance of God's glory and the exact representation of his being, sustaining all things by his powerful word.
> Hebrews 1:2–3 NIV

The Gospels make abundantly clear that Jesus shared our human condition, sufferings, and death. He was fully human. But he was more than human. His resurrection showed that he shared the nature of God Almighty. The gospel, says Paul, concerns God's Son, "who was descended from David according to the flesh and designated Son of God in power according to the Spirit of holiness by his resurrection from the dead, Jesus Christ our Lord" (Rom. 1:3–4). So not only is Brown wildly up the creek about the Council of Nicaea, but it is plain that the teaching that Jesus was divine as well as human goes right back to the New Testament, a quarter of a millennium earlier than Brown maintains! No wonder he won't give television interviews on the book.

Let nobody persuade you that the first Christians did not believe in the divinity of Jesus.

Did the four Gospels become authoritative only in the fourth century?

Brown maintains that the fourth-century emperor Constantine and his associates "commissioned and financed a new Bible," which, by insisting on Jesus's divinity, could enable Constantine to "use his influence to solidify his own power base." He claims that in so doing they ditched the original Gospel material, of which fragments remain in the Gnostic Library at Nag Hammadi in Egypt. We will look at both that claim and these Gnostic gospels in a minute. But for now let's see how his claim about our Gospels being fourth-century productions stands up.

It is, in fact, ignorant rubbish! We have an unorthodox fragment that nevertheless contains clear quotations from all four canonical Gospels as early as AD 120 (*Egerton Papyrus 2*). It is obvious that, if you wanted to get a hearing for unorthodox opinions, you had better quote those recognized as authoritative. Similarly *The Gospel of Truth*, so called, written by a heretic called Valentinus about AD 130, recognizes and depends on all four of our Gospels—with heretical manipulations. Justin, the philosophical Christian writer, in his *First Apology* (*c*. AD 140) speaks of the "memoirs of the apostles," which he says are called Gospels and are read in church alongside the prophets. Tatian was his pupil and around AD 150 produced his *Diatessaron*, which is an (orthodox) attempt to blend all four of our Gospels into one single account.

The publication of Marcion's "canon" around AD 140, accepting only Paul's letters and the Gospel of Luke, caused a fierce reaction in the church and prompted them to make it abundantly clear that it had always held our four Gospels, and them alone, to be authoritative. Then the Muratorian Canon emerged about AD 180 with a nearly complete list of our New Testament, including, of course, all four Gospels by name. The great bishop Irenaeus, with extensive experience in both the East and the West, wrote an important book, *Against Heresies*, at much the same time and makes plain that the norm of orthodox belief is our four Gospels, which he names. He is so clear about the fourfold structure of the Gospel record and their universal recognition that he quaintly compares them to the four winds and the four points of the compass. He sees them as "the four pillars of the church, breathing immortality from every quarter and kindling human life anew" (*Against Heresies* 3.11.8). He then warns against trying to increase or reduce the number of the Gospels.

Finally, it is worth pointing out that we possess partial copies of each of the four Gospels written by AD 150, and a few years after that, complete manuscripts of all the four Gospels bound together in one volume. To cap it all off, we have in the John Rylands Library in Manchester a papyrus fragment of the Gospel of John written not much later than AD 100.

I am not aware how much Dan Brown knows about New Testament origins or how much he is trying to suppress. In either case he merely displays his ignorance, and nobody should be conned by *The Da Vinci Code* or any similar book into supposing that our Gospels were published later than claimed or are fabrications. The second-century church was passionate about retaining, amidst the welter of literary productions of dubious parentage, only those documents, especially Gospels, that could be traced confidently back to the original apostles of Jesus. They were determined to drink only the pure water from the mouth of the stream before it got infected by flowing down the hillside.

Are the Gnostic writings more reliable than the New Testament?

If the date of the canonical Gospels is so early, you may well ask where Brown and his like got their ideas from. They did not spring from thin air but from a remarkable collection of documents found in an ancient jar at Nag Hammadi in Egypt. They were written in Coptic between the third and fifth centuries AD. This is the source for Brown's allegations. At one point his leading character, Teabing, pulls out a big book called *The Gnostic Gospels*, purporting to be "photocopies of the Nag Hammadi and Dead Sea Scrolls ... the earliest Christian records. Troublingly, they do not match up with the Gospels in the Bible."

What a catalog of errors! Or shall we call it poetic license? There is no book combining photocopies of Nag Hammadi and the Dead Sea Scrolls. And the Dead Sea Scrolls contain nothing whatever about Jesus or Christian origins, for the very good reason that they were written before his time! Moreover, the Gnostic gospels were far from being the earliest Christian records. They were late and not very Christian. None of them were written before the second century, long after our Gospels were recognized as authoritative. The existing Coptic copies of Greek originals are put together in a chaotic way with many gaps in the text, sometimes by scribes who clearly did not understand what they were doing. Such texts provide an insecure basis for speculation! We will look at the two texts to which Brown refers.

The Gospel of Philip

Dan Brown attempts to base his idea of Mary Magdalene being the wife of Jesus on a passage from *The Gospel of Philip*. He writes: "And the companion of the Savior is Mary Magdalene. Christ loved her more than all the disciples and used to kiss her often on the mouth. The rest of the disciples were offended by it and expressed disapproval. They said to him 'Why do you love her more than all of us?' "[26]

The actual text is full of gaps. What it says is: "As for the Wisdom who is called 'the barren' she is the mother . . . angels. And the companion of the . . . Mary Magdalene . . . her more than the disciples . . . kiss her on her . . . The rest of . . . They said to him, 'Why do you love her more than all of us?' "

So you can see at once how much is Brown's guesswork. Remember we have only one incomplete fourth-century Coptic copy of *The Gospel of Philip*, and that is full of gaps and missing pages! What a contrast to the four Gospels. We have some five thousand manuscripts of them, drawn from all over the world, and the text is so complete and solid that nobody dares to suggest any alterations. Actually *The Gospel of Philip* isn't a gospel at all as we know it. It has hardly any sayings or stories about Jesus and is rambling and disjointed. It goes on and on about the mysteries of the bridal chamber and distinguishes between those who may participate—freemen and virgins—and those who may not—animals, slaves, and women defiled by sexual intercourse. It refers to God as a "flesh-eater" because human sacrifice is made to him! All very odd. And even if the original text did say that Jesus kissed Mary often, would that be so terrible? Kissing was not—and is not—necessarily a

26. Extract from *The Gospel of Philip* in James M. Robinson, ed., *The Nag Hammadi Library* (Brill, 1988).

sexual act. Doesn't the New Testament say, "Greet one another with a holy kiss"?

The Gospel of Mary

The other source on which Brown draws is the so-called *Gospel of Mary*.

It is fragmentary and the text has yawning gaps. It was written in the early third century and you can see a small fragment of the Greek version in the John Rylands Library, Manchester. For the rest of the document, we have to rely on a single and very incomplete Coptic text from the fourth century. In it, Mary (Magdalene) is recounting a vision of the Savior, which the disciples did not know about. Though much of her discourse is missing, it seems to be saying that sin in the world is due to mixing the material with the spiritual—a typical Gnostic belief. When she finishes, Andrew says, "I for one do not believe that the Savior said this. For certainly these teachings are strange ideas." Then Peter says, "Did He really speak with a woman without our knowledge and not openly? Are we to turn about and all listen to her? Did He prefer her to us?"

And Levi answered and said to Peter, "Peter, you have always been hot tempered. Now I see you contending against the woman like an adversary. But if the Savior made her worthy, who are you to reject her? Surely the Savior knows her very well. That is why He loved her more than us."[27]

From this, Brown's character, Teabing, claims that "according to these unaltered Gospels it was not Peter to whom Christ gave directions with which to establish the Christian Church. It was *Mary Magdalene*."

Sophie exclaimed, "You're saying that the Christian Church was to be carried on by a woman?"

27. Extract from *The Gospel of Mary* in James M. Robinson, ed., *The Nag Hammadi Library* (Brill, 1988).

"That was the plan. Jesus was the original feminist. He intended the future of his church to be in the hands of Mary Magdalene."

Wonderful stuff, isn't it? But there is not a single word, not the suspicion of a hint—even in *The Gospel of Mary*—to suggest any such thing. What it actually shows is one of the major tensions between Gnosticism and Christianity. Peter and Andrew represent orthodox positions that deny the validity of Gnostic claims to secret revelations not found in the apostolic Gospels and reject the authority of women to teach. Not surprisingly, the Gnostic *Gospel of Mary* attacks both positions head-on.

We have seen enough, I think, to laugh at Brown's claim that these Gnostic gospels were unaltered and original. They represented a mixture between Christianity and secular thought stretching from the second to the fourth century.

What did the Gnostics believe?

Gnostic means "the one who has knowledge," knowledge that is hidden from the ordinary Christian whom they despised. You were saved, the Gnostics taught, not by Christ but by "knowledge" (*gnosis*) of Gnostic truth. And what was that? Well, they had a dualistic view of the universe, which saw the body and all physical things as evil, made by an inferior deity. And then there was the spiritual Good God for whom they, hopefully, were headed. There were various magical and mystical ways of getting through to God if you were one of the "elect" Gnostics. You had to be "in the know." Salvation was not by Christ but by knowledge. They wrote off the body; it was a mere envelope for the soul. This led to one or other of two opposite extremes that we find in the Gnostic writings. If you regard matter as an evil prison for your divine spark, there are obviously a couple of ways you can play it. You can either go for hair shirts, beds of broken glass to sleep on, and all other ways of trying to mortify the flesh, or else you can say, "It is my immortal soul that matters. My body is irrelevant (or evil). Nothing I do with it on earth can imperil my heavenly destiny. So let's go out, eat, drink, and fornicate." Both views were enthusiastically undertaken in the second and third centuries by the various Gnostic groups, who hated each other as much as they hated orthodoxy.

Why did they prove a danger to genuine Christianity? Partly because of their belief that the body is bad and the spirit is good. Partly because they sought salvation by magic and mystic routes that sidelined Jesus. Partly because of their immorality. Partly because of their arrogant sectarianism and dangerous theosophy. The decay was beginning to set in during New Testament times. Paul in Colossians and Corinthians, and John in his letters had to contend with it. For Christian salvation is not merely an individual but a corporate rescue: it is concerned with the whole person and not just the soul; it is not the privilege of a select few but open to everyone; and most emphatically, it does not exempt us from the claims either of morality or charity. Gnosticism embraced a dangerous group of heresies. No wonder the church fathers denounced it so passionately. Books like *Holy Blood, Holy Grail* and *The Da Vinci Code*, and films like *The Last Temptation of Christ* all quite deliberately draw from this late and corrupt pool of Gnostic writings. It is not source material for Christian origins at all; it is a corruption of Christianity, a hodgepodge of nonsense, and nobody should be taken in by it. Significantly, not a single orthodox New Testament writing is contained in the jars that held the Gnostic finds at Nag Hammadi. It is a world away from real Christianity. As the church fathers put it, you can't mix honey with poison!

Did Mary Magdalene marry Jesus and have a baby?

Christians know that marriage is a wonderful gift from God; there is no *a priori* reason why Jesus should not have gotten married. But the evidence is decisive that he chose to remain single, as many great spiritual leaders have done.

What do we know about Mary Magdalene? Her name suggests that she came from Magdala on the west coast of the Sea of Galilee. There must have been a time in her life when she was desperate. Jesus cast no less than seven demons out of her (Mark 16:9; Luke 8:2). She was, Luke says, one of a group of women who accompanied Jesus and helped him financially in his ministry. Clearly she was very closely associated with him. We read that she stood by the cross with Mary the mother of Jesus and another Mary, the wife of Clopas (John 19:25). As a matter of fact, all four Gospels tell us that Mary Magdalene was there at the cross, and all four tell us that she was the first to see the risen Jesus on Easter Day. She wanted to hold on to him, but Jesus told her that those days were over; he was about to return to the heavenly Father. She had gone with other women friends to the tomb to anoint Jesus's body, but when it was clear that Jesus had risen from the tomb, she went with them to tell the apostles. But the claim was so stupendous that "these words seemed to them an idle tale, and they did not believe them" (Luke 24:11). We do not know for sure if she was the same Mary, from Bethany, who anointed Jesus's feet with precious ointment before his arrest and wiped them with her hair (John 12:3–7). Nor can we be sure if she was the penitent woman whose deep sins had been forgiven and in gratitude burst in on a supper party and anointed his head (Luke 7:37–50). But on any showing she was one of the closest and most celebrated of all Jesus's disciples. The Eastern Church calls her "the apostle to the apostles" because she was charged by Jesus with giving them first news of the resurrection.

What became of her we do not know. According to Eastern tradition, she accompanied the apostle John to Ephesus where she died and was buried. An eleventh-century tradition spuriously claims that she evangelized Provence and lived in a cave in the Alps. Medieval legend has it that she became the apostle John's wife. But we do not know.

What we can be pretty sure about is that Brown is wrong in claiming that Mary Magdalene was the "sacred feminine" suppressed by the male leadership of the Roman Church. The world is full of churches in her honor, not to mention two colleges in Oxford and Cambridge! But he is right in saying that she had a great following, particularly among Gnostics in the second and third centuries. We have already seen how she figures in *The Gospel of Mary* and *The Gospel of Philip*. *The Gospel of Thomas*, the earliest and best of the gospels found at Nag Hammadi, written in the second century, has her as a close companion of Jesus and makes her an honorary man! In the final words of the gospel, Peter says to Jesus, "Let Mary leave us, for women are not worthy of life." Jesus replies, "I myself shall lead her in order to make her male, so that she too may become a living spirit resembling you males!" But most of the Gnostics were obsessed with femininity and saw her as superior to the men and the channel of secret revelations so dear to Gnostic hearts.

Sorry to disappoint you, but the idea that she married Jesus and they had a baby girl has no evidence anywhere in all of history to support it! It is a late twentieth-century fable. It is a flight of Brown's imagination. After all, he is a novelist! I wonder if he knows that in the nineteenth century Brigham Young, the founder of the Mormons, maintained that among his many wives Jesus had Mary, Martha, and Mary Magdalene? He had a vivid imagination too!

Now here's something. An American TV station in the summer of 2004 conducted a survey on whether the viewers believed that Jesus and Mary Magdalene were married and had a child but the church kept it secret. A stunning 34 percent said they did believe it. My friend Dr. Ward Gasque reminds me of G. K. Chesterton's famous comment: "When men cease to believe in God they do not believe in nothing: they believe in anything!"

6

"It doesn't matter what you believe as long as you are sincere."

Attractive but wrong

Lots of people seem to believe this. And it is certainly a very attractive position to hold. For one thing it is eminently tolerant; and tolerance is just about the only virtue that has escaped the corroding cynicism of our day. It sounds like a very liberal and enlightened creed, for it means that everyone will win the race, and everyone will get prizes.

There is another reason for its appeal. At a stroke it removes the problem of seeking the truth, the embarrassment of being challenged by it. And that is very agreeable. After all, we are so busy these days we have little time to examine the different religions of the world, and we have no desire to have our lives unmasked by the truth when we find it.

What's more, this view that it doesn't matter what you believe as long as you are sincere has the great advantage of giving voice to our deep-seated disgust at insincerity. It is always a blow when an individual or a country loudly professes one thing and then promptly does another. But perhaps the worst kind of insincerity is the religious kind. The corruption of the Tsarist Church in nineteenth-century Russia, for example, was positively scandalous. Again, in the last century in England, thousands of workingmen went to church in order to keep in good favor with the bosses, not because they were believing Christians. We have no time for insincerity like that. And when occasionally one hears of a church organization charging excessive rents from the poor, or a bishop in an adulterous relationship, we feel swindled and let down. We say, "It doesn't matter what people believe as long as they are sincere."

But, attractive though it is, it will not do. If you tell me that you believe it, I shall conclude—you can't be serious! Here are three good reasons why I can't accept it.

Life teaches us that sincerity is not enough

A moment's reflection will show what a ludicrous creed it is! We would never apply it to matters we consider important, would we? Take politics, for instance. What politician would accept for a moment that it does not matter what you believe as long as you are sincere? That would obliterate the difference between Monarchist and Republican, between Socialist and Conservative, between Nationalist and Progressive. On that view it would be impossible to censure Iraq's invasion of Kuwait. On that view you could whitewash Hitler's ruthless slaughter of six million Jews in pursuit of the *Herrenvolk* (Master Race) policy! No, in politics it matters enormously what you believe.

We would never apply this argument about sincerity being enough to economics, say, or to examinations. Who could suppose that it doesn't matter what firm you invest your money in as long as you sincerely believe that it is sound? Who would maintain that it does not matter what you believe when you write a thesis? You can put down sense or nonsense; it makes no difference, as long as you are sincere! As we all know to our cost, you can be very sincere and very wrong.

Actually, you'd never get to work in the morning if you operated on this sincerity principle. No matter what earnest beliefs you held about the public transport system, you would miss your train and fail to reach your destination if you took no notice of the timetable but continued to maintain that it does not matter what people believe as long as they are sincere.

Pause to reflect on it for a moment. The outlook we have been considering is not only merely ridiculous, but it is also cruel. Just think of applying it to advising someone trying to cross a busy road: "It doesn't matter what you believe about the speed and frequency of cars. Just carry on sincerely toward the other side, and you'll be all right!" Liberal and tolerant though it seemed to begin with, this outlook turns out to be cynical and cruel. Under the guise of charity, this maxim hides a callous indifference to truth. It is little short of criminal.

Yes, life teaches us unequivocally that it matters enormously what we believe. We need to be sincere; we also need to be right.

The Bible teaches us that sincerity is not enough

Now, you may or may not be inclined to take the Bible as a final authority on God. But you must at least recognize that it is the most significant book in the world, has done more than any other book to change the world for good, remains the world's best seller, and was composed over a period of some fifteen hundred years. So it may be worth listening to. It may well embody perspective and wisdom, for it comprises a very broad spectrum of human history and experience. What does it have to say on whether sincerity is enough?

Take, first, a man like Abraham, the father of the Jewish nation. If you were to ask him whether sincerity was enough, he would reply, "Far from it. I was sincere when I lived in Ur of the Chaldeans. But God called me out. I believed him and obeyed. God promised to raise up a family and, indeed, a nation out of my loins, when both my wife and I were too old to have children. I believed him—and here is Isaac my son to show you how much belief matters. Why, the whole latter part of my life has been based on the conviction that what you believe is fundamental to what you do and what you are." What Abraham became in virtue of his faith in God is graphically summarized in Hebrews 11:8–19 (if you find the longer account, starting in Genesis 14, too much to cope with).

Deborah, the prophetess who delivered Israel from the Canaanites in the days of the Judges, would never have agreed that it does not matter what you believe as long as you are sincere. Her general, Barak, sincerely believed that they were no match for the enemy, and by her faith and courage she showed him that he was wrong. She won a mighty victory over King Jabin and his Canaanite hordes, and the land had rest for forty years as a result (Judges 4–5).

Naaman, the great Syrian general and a leper, was a stickler for sincerity. He sincerely believed that Elisha the prophet would come out to him "and stand, and call on the name of the LORD his God, and wave his hand over the place, and cure the leper" (2 Kings 5:11). He sincerely believed that if washing in a river was to be the prescription, the cool, clear waters of his native Abana and Pharpar would do every bit as much good as Israel's muddy Jordan. He was sincere, but wrong. If he had not admitted as much and changed his attitude, he would never have been healed (see 2 Kings 5:1–14).

The night of the Exodus, when the escape of the Israelites from Egypt cemented them fully into a nation, was another case in point. You may recall the story, found in Exodus 12. Only those households that sacrificed a lamb and splashed some of its blood above the doorpost of their home were spared the death of their firstborn. Only they left Egypt unharmed. If a father had said, "Oh, it doesn't matter about that silly old blood on the lintel. Let's get a good night's sleep in preparation for the journey," he might well have been sincere, but he'd have been wrong; his firstborn son would have been dead, and there would have been no Promised Land for him.

The New Testament attitude is the same. The Pharisees are the outstanding examples of people, highly religious people at that, who thought they were OK—and they were not. Pontius Pilate seems to have been a fairly sincere governor of a difficult province—Judea; he may well have believed it would be in the general interest for Jesus to be liquidated, but he was wrong. Saul of Tarsus believed he could put himself in the right with God by meticulously keeping the law and zealously persecuting the heretics—but he came to realize that his sincere attempt was a hopeless failure. Saul, the fanatical, self-righteous persecutor, who became Paul, the dedicated, loving apostle, is a splendid example of the fact that sincerity is not enough. It matters what you believe.

Jesus teaches us that sincerity is not enough
It would be difficult to find anyone more sincere than the rich young ruler; but we read that he went away sorrowful, because he did not believe enough in Jesus to give him priority over his money (Luke 18:18–24).

Nobody could have been more sincere than the Pharisees. They were meticulous in their worship, fastidious in keeping clear of any defilement, and dedicated to keeping the law of God. They were sincere, but wrong. It was these very Pharisees whom Jesus had to describe as a viper's brood; it was they who, he observed, "refuse to come to me to have life" (John 5:40 NIV). Sincere in their practice, they were mistaken in their belief, and Jesus was more stringent in his condemnation of those dedicated, sincere men than of the traitors and the prostitutes whom they despised. It does matter what you believe. So much so that when the Jews, anxious to please God by *doing* something, came and asked Jesus, "What does God want us to do?" he replied, "This is what God wants you to do—*Believe* in the one he has sent" (John 6:28–29 NLT, emphasis added).

Sincerity and belief

Nowhere in the Gospels does Jesus stress more powerfully the supreme importance of belief than in the best-known verse of the whole Bible: "God so loved the world that he gave his only Son, that whoever believes in him should not perish but have eternal life" (John 3:16). The passage continues:

> He who believes in him is not condemned; he who does not believe is condemned already, because he has not believed in the name of the only Son of God. And this is the judgment, that the light has come into the world, and men loved darkness rather than light, because their deeds were evil.
>
> John 3:18–20

God, you see, not sincerity, is the supreme reality. And God saw that we were perishing, on the way to final ruin, because it is all too easy to be sincere, and wrong. So God did something about it. He sent Jesus, who was one with himself and yet distinct from himself; "son" is maybe the best human analogy. Jesus lived and died for the express purpose of rescuing us and enabling us to enjoy a new quality of life, eternal life.

There is just one condition. We are called to believe! Jesus goes on to make it plain that we will not be ruined by our evil ways, which, to some extent, we cannot help. We will be ruined by failing to trust the one who has brought the remedy for our sick condition. The Light has come into the world. The bridge back to God has been established. It is up to us to believe or reject; we have the choice, and we shall be held responsible for our decision. "He who believes in him is not condemned"; no, for Jesus has borne his condemnation. "But he who does not believe is condemned already," not because he is a sinner (which he is) but because he has been fool enough to reject the remedy. Do not, I beg you, commit this ultimate folly under the claim of tolerance. If there happens to be only one antitoxin for a disease, it is not charity but folly to say, "It doesn't matter whether you take it or not as long as you are sincere." And we all have the disease. It has affected our past. It dogs our present. It threatens our future.

The limitations of sincerity

Can sincerity change the past? I think of a gangster who found Christ in prison—and I can see him now, out of prison, reconciled with his wife, accepted and loved in a Christian community. He has been released from his past. Sincerity could never produce a change like that. Only Jesus can. Belief in Jesus puts you in touch with the one who died to clean up your past. "There is therefore now no condemnation for those who are in Christ Jesus" (Rom. 8:1).

Can sincerity change a person's life in the present? I think of an obsessive gambler who had tried everything to break the habit, and had failed. He discovered that sincerity is not enough. And then he came to Christ. The Spirit of Jesus came into his life, and at once the old slavery to gambling was broken. Not so surprising after all, is it? You'd expect Jesus to make a difference, and he does. I think of a couple whose marriage was breaking up, though they had sincerely tried to make a go of it. But once they both came to terms with Christ and welcomed his Spirit into their lives, they found each other afresh and are now living happy and useful Christian lives.

Or think of the future. Can sincerity set our minds at rest about death and what follows death? Anyone who has attended the dying knows that it cannot. But the one who rose from the dead, the one who "holds the keys of death and the afterlife," can take away the dread of death and hell. I think of an old friend of mine, a bishop in China, who for years had been the director of one of the biggest missionary agencies in the world. When his time came to die, he asked for the Hallelujah Chorus from Handel's *Messiah* to be played, and his request was granted. He then murmured, "Wonderful!" and passed joyfully into his Master's presence. Like Handel, like

Christians all down the ages, he pinned his faith for the future not in sincerity or tolerance but in the Risen One.

Do you see now why belief is so important? The Lord offers us so much: the cross to lift the burden of the past; the Spirit to change the selfishness of our lives; the resurrection to assure us of a future with him. Three firm, objective realities—no mere sincerity. No wonder the Reformers in the sixteenth century used to rejoice in three great mottoes:

- *Sola gratia*—by God's free goodness alone
- *Sola fide*—through faith alone
- *Soli Deo gloria*—and to God alone be the glory!

Incidentally, aren't you glad that we are not judged by our sincerity? What a burden that would impose on every minute of the day, on the motivation of every action, on the expression of every word. The word "sincere" comes from the Latin *sine cera*, "without wax." It is a metaphor derived from bee-keeping. Quality honey has to be wax free, and the Greek word for "sincere," which literally means "judged in the light of the sun," shows how you decided the matter. Why, if I were judged in the blazing sunlight of God's holiness, and my every word and deed and motive was scrutinized for sincerity, I wouldn't have a hope. Would you? I'm all too aware of insincerity in myself and others to relish a test like that. "How nice to see you," we say, when inwardly furious at the interruption. "I haven't the time," we say, when faced with something we don't want to do. "What about those who have never heard the gospel?" we ask, when the wonder and challenge of what Christ has done drives us into a corner. Shallow insincerities, all of them! Even the glib claim that sincerity is all we need itself reeks of insincerity. We do not apply it to any other area of life; it is just an excuse to evade facing up to the light.

When I am confronted by the God who is too holy to tolerate evil in those he loves, the God whose eyes are like flaming fire—

then I am thankful that I shall have something more substantial than sincerity to rely on. I shall be resting my weight on the Jesus in whom I have believed. How about you?

Four questions, as I close this chapter.

Why is believing so important?

For two good reasons. Partly, because belief is the basis for action. It is foolish to concentrate on sincerity of action if you are casual about the nature of your beliefs. What you believe leads inevitably to what you do and what you are.

But there is an even more important answer to this question. Believing is so important, because it is the only conceivable response to love. When God's love is brought to me in Christ, I merely insult him if I say, "Right, that's very nice of you. Now how about a bit of churchgoing, a bit of sincerity and turning over a new leaf so as to earn your love?" The only proper response to such a generous and undeserved gift is to stretch out the hand of faith and say "Thank you."

What does believing achieve?

Once again, the answer can be roughly summarized in two parts. First, it clears up the past, or rather claims the clearing up that Christ achieved on the cross. "Since we are justified by faith, we have peace with God," was Paul's triumphant discovery (Rom. 5:1). It's as if I were in prison and, all unknown to me, a pardon from the governor was being drawn up for me. I would stay in prison, along with my accusing record, until I accepted that governor's pardon and stepped out, a freeman with nothing against my name.

Second, believing brings a person into God's family. "To all who received him, to those who believed in his name, he gave the right to become children of God," says John (John 1:12 NIV). Paul says we have received the Spirit who adopts us into the family (see Rom. 8:15). It is as though we were juvenile delinquents, and the judge not only settled our fine himself but also adopted us into his family alongside his own son. There is nothing we could do to earn it. We would just trustingly accept the new relationship, say "Thank you," and try to live lives worthy of it.

What will believing involve?

It is certainly no cheap option, no easy alternative to costly action. But neither does believing mean that we are committed to endless dreary and legalistic observances. Look at it like this. What will believing in his coach mean to the athlete? What will believing in his teacher mean to the pupil? What will believing in her doctor mean for the patient? What will believing in the parent mean for the child or believing in the husband mean for the wife? Certainly discipline and obedience will be part of the total package; but somehow it will not be irksome, because of the relationship. That is what it is like to believe in Jesus. It is a lifelong commitment, a dependence on and an ever-growing obedience to the one who has shown himself to be utterly reliable. Because he came to this world in order to seek me; because he died for me and rose for me; because he offers to share my very life and enter the inmost recesses of my being, I know I can trust him to the fullest. And what is belief, if not trust?

How do I actually believe?

Once again, there are two parts to it. Having got past the stage of thinking that faith is believing what you know is not true, or that it consists in reciting the creeds in a parrotlike fashion, it resolves itself into a matter for the head and a matter for the will.

Let's look at the intellectual side first. Belief is no surrender of the intellect. It is no blind acceptance of everything in the Bible or every dogma of the Christian church. No. Belief is concerned with Jesus Christ. If you like, Jesus is God's right hand of fellowship stretched out to us. Belief is our hand of response, stretched out to him. The two need to meet. I ask you, then, do you believe that Jesus Christ is the Son of God? Do you believe he died for you? Do you believe he is the risen Lord, willing and able to change your life? That is the hard core of Christian belief. The early Christians summarized it in the famous fish symbol—for the five letters that make up the Greek word for fish could be seen as the first letters of the following claims about Jesus: "Jesus Christ, Son of God, Savior." Those claims take you to the nerve center of Christian belief.

But it is all too easy to believe things in your head without getting personally involved with them or acting on them. That is why it is vital to realize that belief is a matter not only of the mind but of the will. This delightful story about Blondin,[28] the celebrated tightrope walker of a hundred years ago, makes the point with humor and clarity. He specialized in crossing the Niagara Falls on a tightrope. Variations included crossing blindfold, swathed in a sack, at night, on stilts, and with his feet tied up in blankets. In 1860 he performed before the then Prince of Wales, who was visiting Niagara as part of a tour. Blondin offered to carry him over on his back. The prince declined but with royal graciousness suggested that the Duke of Newcastle, who was in attendance, might like to accept. Unfortunately, the Duke of Newcastle too refused!

Now these two men believed, in the intellectual sense, that Blondin could do it, but this was not faith in the full-blooded New Testament sense of the word. There was no act of will, no personal commitment. By way of contrast, Blondin's mother watched him wheel a sack of potatoes over the falls, and then, at his suggestion, climbed into the wheelbarrow herself and entrusted herself to his skill and balance. She was not disappointed. That is a good example of authentic faith.

How about you and Jesus Christ? Do you believe in him with your head? Then put yourself at his disposal. Climb into that

28. Blondin's real name was Jean François Gravelet (1824–1897).

wheelbarrow, so to speak, and tell him that you realize sincerity is not enough, that you entrust your life to him, and that you don't mind who knows it.

A genuine act of self-surrender like that will give birth to a growing conviction that Christ, not mere sincerity, is what you need in this life and the next. For the act of commitment leads on to a life of companionship with him who makes all things new—even for you.

7

"All religions lead to God."

An attractive theory

Until a few years ago, comparative religion was a study for the handful of experts who busied themselves in such an odd subject. Now it is replacing the study of theology in universities all over the Western world and has a firm niche in religious instruction in schools. The reason, of course, is that we have at last woken up to the fact that the world is a global village, bringing the question of other religions much closer. What are we to make of these other faiths? Presumably they are all very much the same. Presumably they are all pathways to God, and you might as well take your pick.

Such a view has immense attractions. It avoids a black-and-white choice and sees everything as shades of gray. It is essentially tolerant, and tolerance is a very fashionable virtue. It is modest and does not make strong pretensions for your own particular religion. It seems admirable common sense. We take the views of everybody and try to build up a composite sketch of God. And some extremely significant people and organizations back it up. For example, the saintly Indian leader Mahatma Gandhi said, "The soul of religions is one, but it is encased in a multitude of forms.... Truth is the exclusive property of no single scripture.... I cannot ascribe exclusive divinity to Jesus. He is as divine as Krishna or Rammer or Mohammed or Zoroaster."[29]

But this view won't do, for two compelling reasons.

29. R. K. Prabhu and U. R. Rao, *The Mind of Mahatma Gandhi* (Greenleaf Books, 1988).

It's illogical

It is a lovely sentiment to suppose that all religions are basically one, and that they represent variations on a common theme. But, unfortunately, it flies in the face of all the evidence. How can all religions lead to God when they are so different? The god of Hinduism is plural and impersonal. The god of Islam is singular and personal. The God of Christianity is the Creator of the world. The divine in Buddhism is not personal and is not creative. You could scarcely have a greater contrast than that. Christianity teaches that God both forgives us and gives us supernatural aid. In Buddhism there is no forgiveness and no supernatural aid. The goal of all existence in Buddhism is *nirvana*, extinction—attained by the Buddha after no less than 547 births. The goal of all existence in Christianity is to know God and enjoy him forever. The use of images figures prominently in Hinduism; Judaism prohibits making any image of God. Islam allows a man four wives; Christianity, one. Perhaps the greatest difference of all lies between the teachings of the Bible—which assert that none of us can save ourselves and make ourselves pleasing to God—and the teachings of almost all the other faiths—which assert that by observing their tenets a person can be saved or reborn or made whole or achieve fulfillment. Nothing spells out this contrast more powerfully than the Buddhist story that starts off much like the parable of the prodigal son. The boy comes home and is met by the father, and then has to work off the penalty for his past misdeeds by years of servitude to his father. The principle of *karma* (cause and effect, paying off your guilt) is poles apart from grace (free forgiveness when you don't deserve it at all).

I do not at this point want to evaluate different religious faiths. I just want to show how utterly illogical it is to say that they are all pointing in the same direction. It is as foolish as to say that all roads from Philadelphia lead to New York City. They do nothing of the sort, and it is not helpful in the least to pretend that they do. They lead to radically different goals.

Extinction or heaven; pardon or paying it off; a personal God or an impersonal being; salvation by grace or by works. The contrasts are irreconcilable.

The trouble is that today's tolerance has reached the point where it is no longer a virtue but a vice. It is a cruel casualness toward truth. It is no kindness to anyone if we tell everyone that their views are as true as anyone else's. We are simply displaying our cynicism, as if we said to a blind person sitting on the edge of a precipice, "It doesn't matter which way you move. All paths lead to the same goal."

Bishop Lesslie Newbigin maintains that the great divide among religions is in their attitude to history. Most religions are like a wheel:

> The cycle of birth, growth, decay and death through which plants, animals, human beings and institutions all pass suggests a rotating wheel—ever in movement yet ever returning upon itself. . . . [So] dispute among the different "ways" is pointless; all that matters is that those who follow them should find their way to that timeless, motionless centre where all is peace, and where one can understand all the endless movement which makes up human history—understand that it goes nowhere and means nothing.[30]

The other great symbol is not a wheel but a road. This is the view of Judaism and Christianity. Newbigin expresses it thus:

> History is a journey, a pilgrimage. We do not yet see the goal, but we believe in it and seek it. The movement in which we are involved is not meaningless movement; it is movement towards a goal. The goal . . . is not a timeless reality hidden behind the multiplicity and change which we experience. It is yet to be achieved; it lies at the end of the road.

That is the uniqueness of the Christian claim. God has intervened in history. The history of the Jewish people, the birth of

30. Lesslie Newbigin, *The Finality of Christ* (SCM, 1968).

Jesus, the cross, and the resurrection are milestones along that road, which ends in heaven.

Not only, then, is it illogical to suppose that all religions lead to God; it is impossible.

The nature of God

There are two reasons why it is impossible for us to find God through whatever religion you care to name. The first is because of the nature of God. If there is a God, then he is the source both of ourselves and of our environment. He is the Lord of all human life:

> Have you not known? Have you not heard?
>   Has it not been told you from the beginning? . . .
> It is he who sits above the circle of the earth,
>   and its inhabitants are like grasshoppers. . . .
> Whom did he consult for his enlightenment,
>   and who taught him the path of justice,
> and taught him knowledge,
>   and showed him the way of understanding?
> Behold, the nations are like a drop from a bucket,
>   and are accounted as the dust on the scales;
>   behold, he takes up the isles like fine dust.
>
> Isaiah 40:21–22, 14–15

That is the God we are talking about. How can we possibly climb up to him? How can the cup understand the potter who made it? It cannot be done. Mere mortals cannot find God, however hard we search. Religion, all religion, is bound to fail.

As we have seen, we can have a go at it. But how far does it get us? The facts we considered in the last chapter get us a little way down the road, but only a very little way, and they amount to not much more than conjecture. The fact of the world indicates an outside cause. Design in the world suggests this cause's intelligence. The fact of human life suggests that this cause is not only intelligent but personal. Conscience indicates his concern about right conduct, and values such as truth, beauty, and goodness may have their origin in him. The fact that no nation in the world has lived without belief in God suggests that God wants our worship.

But so what? He remains the unknown God. You can get only so far by inference, but no farther. After that you need to hear from him, or meet him—or both. The creature cannot possibly discover the Creator, unless he chooses to disclose himself. That is one reason why all religions are bound to disappoint. And, as a matter of fact, that is precisely what they all do.

Christopher Mayhew published a book some years ago, entitled *Men in Search of God*. In it, representatives of various world religions gave their account of their religious experience and their search for God. Not surprisingly, none of them claimed to have found him. Gordon Bailey puts it epigrammatically in his little poem "If":

> If
> all religions
> lead to God
> how come
> most of them,
> having been given
> a thousand years at least,
> haven't yet
> arrived?[31]

If by "religion" we mean our search for the divine, it is bound to fail. What we need is not to compare the chinks of light that each of us may have grasped but for the day to dawn. We need not a religion but a revelation. And that is precisely what Christianity claims to be. A revelation from God. Unlike other holy books, the Bible does not pretend that we are seeking God;

31. Gordon Bailey, *Patchwork Quill*, publisher unknown.

it tells us about the God who comes in search of us. You could
fairly rename the Bible *God in search of man*!

The nature of man

There is a second reason why religion will never win through to
God. Not simply because of the nature of God but because of
the nature of man. The Bible gives a pretty unflattering picture
of men and women, but one that is uncomfortably near the
mark. It tells us several unpleasant truths.

For instance, it informs us that we are not the earnest lovers
of God that we would like to suppose; on the contrary, we are
"hostile in mind, doing evil deeds" (Col. 1:21). We do not have
that heart of gold, which we like to think we have; on the
contrary, "the heart [of man] is deceitful above all things, and
desperately corrupt" (Jer. 17:9). The Bible tells us that we are
not impartial in our search for the truth; on the contrary,
people "suppress the truth by their wickedness" (Rom. 1:18
NIV). We do not follow every gleam of light that comes our
way; on the contrary, people "loved darkness rather than light,
because their deeds were evil" (John 3:19).

There seems to be a basic twist in human nature that makes
us incapable of welcoming the best when we see it. More often
than not, we want to get rid of it because it shows us up. One
of the more pathetic illusions of humanism is that we are good
folk at heart and, given plenty of money and secure employment, we will all be good citizens, and the heart of gold will
shine out. What rubbish! If we are all good folk at heart,
why does the crime rate go up every year, along with our
prosperity? If we were all good folk at heart, we would flock to
the best person there has ever been, Jesus Christ. But anyone
who has ever helped a friend to start the Christian life knows
what a battle generally ensues before the person in question
finally gives in to Christ. I have seen "good" people sweating
with the intensity of their struggle to keep clear of the Light of
the World. Francis Thompson knew what he was talking

about in that poem of his, "The Hound of Heaven," which begins:

> I fled Him, down the nights and down the days;
>   I fled Him, down the arches of the years;
> I fled Him, down the labyrinthine ways
>   Of my own mind; and in the mist of tears
> I hid from Him, and under running laughter.[32]

The very fact that we hide from him shows that we are self-centered creatures at heart, just as the Bible says we are. And we have another closely allied problem. There is something wrong with our will. We don't seem to be able to live up even to our own occasional efforts of committing to high standards. How long do your New Year's resolutions last, for instance? How long does that peace and goodwill of the Christmas period continue in your office? Or how many times have you tried to stop overeating? Jesus put his finger on the trouble when he said, "Everyone who sins is a slave to sin" (John 8:34 NIV).

No wonder Paul comes to the same conclusion that the Old Testament had reached before him, as he draws to the end of his shattering indictment of contemporary pagan and religious society. "None is righteous, no, not one; no one understands, no one seeks for God" (Rom. 3:10–11). The myth is exploded. We are not honest seekers after God. Most of us, most of the time, are only too thankful to keep out of his way. All of us are disqualified, whether we come from the so-called Christian West, the collapsed Communist bloc, or the mystic East. None have arrived at God, because he is too great for any of his creatures to reach him and because his creatures are too twisted, too self-centered to want to reach him. The greatness of God and human sinfulness are two massive barriers to our supposing that all religions lead to God. All religions do not lead to God. None of them do.

32. Francis Thompson, *The Works of Francis Thompson, Poems*, 2 vols. (Charles Scribner's Sons, 1913).

Only one hope

There is only one hope, and that is the possibility of revelation. We cannot reach God, but there is no reason why he should not reach us. That is a consideration that escaped the celebrated Herbert Spencer, a leading agnostic. He maintained, sensibly enough, that no one has ever been known to penetrate with his finite mind the veil that hides the mind of the Infinite. He concluded that the Infinite could not be known by the finite, and that agnosticism was therefore secure. But there was a fatal flaw in his argument. There is no reason why the Infinite should not make himself known to the finite, and the Bible gives the account of the only faith that claims that he has done precisely that.

A revelation

Suppose for a moment you were God. The people you had made have turned their backs on you. They do not want to share their lives with you. They want to go their own way. What are you to do? You might start with a likely individual and work on him and his descendants. God did just that: the likely individual was called Abraham. He trusted God, obeyed him, and became the father of the Jewish nation. But that nation strayed away from the path Abraham had trodden. What was to be done? Perhaps a time of hardship in a foreign and oppressive country might make them come to their senses. That is what Israel's time in Egypt was all about, and later on the medicine had to be repeated in the Babylonian exile. You might raise up prophets to call the people back to yourself. God did just that too: "Though the Lord has sent all his servants the prophets to you again and again, you have not listened or paid any attention" (Jer. 25:4 NIV).

Finally, if you cared enough, you might come in person, for a sort of summit visit, after your staff had sufficiently prepared the way. That too God did at the first Christmas. The way was as prepared as it could be. The Jewish nation, after two thousand years of history, was passionately persuaded that there was one God, and no runners up. The Roman Empire had secured peace throughout the known world. The Greek language was universal and its culture pervasive. The stage was set for the maximum impact of God's personal visit. And so the one called Jesus ("God the rescuer"), or Emmanuel ("God is with us"), was born. The God who, over many centuries and in many different ways, had spoken through his prophets to the people, had at last spoken a clear, final and decisive message, not through a prophet but in the person of his Son. At long last men and women could see that God is, God speaks, God cares. No longer is he the unknown God. "No one has ever seen God, but God the One and Only, who is at the Father's side, has made him known," was how one eyewitness summed the matter up (John 1:18 NIV). Jesus shows us in terms of a human life what God is like. That was the first purpose of his coming to our world, to bring us the revelation of God without which we would still be fumbling vainly in the dark.

A rescue

His coming had a second purpose as well, closely linked with the first. For when human beings saw that perfect life of uprightness and love, the highest and the best imaginable, they nailed him to a cross. He was too uncomfortable. His was too blazing a light. The natural instinct of humankind, who likes living in the dark, was—and is—to extinguish that embarrassing light. They did not succeed, of course. "The light shines in the darkness, and the darkness has not overcome it" (John 1:5), but they made an excellent attempt. Do you see what happened? The coming of Jesus did not merely show us what God is like. It also showed up what we are like. "Men loved darkness rather than light, because their deeds were evil," wrote John (John 3:19); and if you want commentary on that verse, ask yourself what would happen to the circulation of the Sunday papers if they started recording acts of virtue rather than deeds of vice! There you have clear evidence that we love darkness rather than light. So we human beings need something more basic even than a revelation from God. We need a rescue by God.

Not only our understanding but our will is at fault. Jesus came to rectify both. He showed us what God was like by his incomparable life. He put us right with God by his sacrificial death. That is why the cross is the symbol of Christianity. It is the most important achievement in the whole of his life, indeed in the whole of history. There Jesus, the God-man, took responsibility for human sin in its totality. "Christ . . . died for sins . . . , the righteous for the unrighteous, to bring [us] to God," says one eyewitness (1 Pet. 3:18). "This is love: not that we loved God, but that he loved us and sent his Son as an atoning sacrifice for our sins," writes another (1 John 4:10 NIV). Wherever you look in the New Testament, you find the same truth, however variously it is expressed. In the pictorial language of the book of Revelation, you find it put like this:

> I looked and there before me was a great multitude that no one could count, from every nation, tribe, people and language, standing before the throne and in front of the Lamb. They were wearing white robes and were holding palm branches in their hands. And they cried out in a loud voice:
>
> > "Salvation belongs to our God,
> > who sits on the throne,
> > and to the Lamb."
>
> Revelation 7:9–10 NIV

Nothing like it

The symbolism is plain. These people, from every background in the world, are praising God in heaven, and thanking him for his rescue operation that covers the scruffy clothes of their fancied goodness with the perfect white robe of Christ's righteousness. As the writer goes on to say, a few verses later:

These are they who . . . have washed their robes and made them white in the blood [i.e., the death] of the Lamb [i.e., Jesus, willingly sacrificed for them].

Revelation 7:14

A rescue operation indeed. Where else in the religions of the world do you hear of a God who undertakes salvation for his people by personally bearing responsibility for their wickedness, allowing it to crush him?

But even that is not all. The God who has revealed himself and rescued us has done it for a purpose. Amazingly, he wants to relate to us. That is where the resurrection comes in. He is no dead figure in a history book, two thousand years out-of-date. He is alive, and we can have dealings with him. I remember vividly the day when this truth became a reality to me. I asked the Risen One to come and live in me. He has done so. I have not found God. I could not if I wanted to, and I would not have wanted to anyway, because I was so self-centered. But he has found me. He came to earth to reveal himself to me. He died to remove the guilt of my wrongdoing. He lives and is at work changing my life from the inside. And all this I find to be very good news.

No other faith does anything remotely like this. No other faith claims to. Christianity is quite distinct from other religions. It is not a case of man in search of God but of God in search of man. Not a religion at all but a revelation and a rescue.

It is at this point that two important questions arise.

"If you are right about Jesus, are other religions all wrong?"

By no means. The God who made the world, the God who revealed himself in Christ, has not left himself without witness in the world. Every good thought, every gleam of light, every word of truth to be found in any religion, and in atheistic philosophies like Marxism as well, is part of God's self-disclosure. All truth is God's truth and has its focus in the one who became incarnate. Christians welcome truth wherever it is found. As you look into other faiths, you will find an enormous amount that is true and worthy, that is moral and good, as well as much that is not. But you will not find anything that is good and true that cannot be found in Christ. You will not hear from them about a God who cares for you enough to die for you, to rise from the grave as a pledge of your future, and to be willing to come and share your life with you. You will not find in any other faith a revelation of God in fully personal terms, a rescue of man from his self-centeredness and sin, and the offer by this God to come and indwell the life of every man, woman, or child who welcomes him.

It is not that Christians are narrow-minded about other faiths. But if Jesus is, as the resurrection asserts, God himself come to our rescue, then it is gross folly to reject him. And this is something that we can investigate for ourselves. We are not dealing with myth and legend, of the sort that makes it impossible to know when Buddha lived (estimates vary between 1000 and 500 BC) or details of his birth (there are many birth stories). We are dealing with history. Christians claim (and there is plenty of documentary evidence to support the claim) that Jesus of Nazareth rose from the dead on the first Easter Day in AD 30 or 31 and launched the Christian community. His scattered followers did not expect it. To begin with, they did not believe it. But they were driven to do so by their experience of the risen Jesus, and once they were convinced, nothing could silence them. For they had discovered the key to life. They did not claim merely that a corpse had been resuscitated. That would not have done much good. They believed that almighty God took our nature as the man Jesus, that he suffered and died, and that death could not hold him (see Acts 2:24)! His resurrection says "Yes" to his claim to be the way, the truth, and the life (see John 14:6). The resurrection vindicates his claim to deity. In the risen Jesus, God confronts us with shattering directness. He offers us total aid, but he demands of us total obedience. It is splendid to have an interest in comparative religion. But the more you know of others, the more you see Christianity to be unique. And the key to Christianity is the resurrection.

I have investigated the reliability of the resurrection with some care in a little book *The Empty Cross of Jesus*, and we shall be looking at the evidence more briefly in chapter 12. But the point is this: Christianity is a historical religion. It claims that God has taken the risk of involving himself in human history, and the evidence is there for you to examine with the utmost rigor. The facts will stand any amount of critical examination. No book on earth has been subjected to as much prolonged and detailed scrutiny by some of the best minds in the world over many hundreds of years as the New Testament. Examine the evidence for yourself, and do not rely on secondhand opinions from those who believe the Christian story or from those who reject it. This is the most important issue you will ever have to decide. Did Jesus rise from the dead or not? If not, then there will be time enough to look to all the other faiths in the world, to see what help for living can be found in them. But if he did rise, and you are persuaded of it, then that settles for you the question of which religion. Christ can no longer appear to you just as a very fine man. Although fully human, he somehow brings God to you. And, as God, he claims your loyal obedience.

The second question that commonly arises at this point is the following.

"If you are right about Jesus, are all non-Christians inevitably lost?"

Here again the answer is no. It is certainly not taught in the New Testament that all who have not heard of Jesus Christ are inevitably lost. The whole Bible makes it plain that men and women will be judged by God with utter fairness, and they will be judged by their response to such light as they have had. In a famous passage of his letter to the Romans, Paul maintains resolutely that God has no favorites:

> When Gentiles who have not the law do by nature what the law requires, they are a law to themselves, even though they do not have the law. They show that what the law requires is written on their hearts, while their conscience also bears witness and their conflicting thoughts accuse or perhaps excuse them on that day when ... God judges the secrets of men by Jesus Christ.
>
> Romans 2:14–16

He means that heathen nations who do not have God's revelation in the Scriptures still have a knowledge of right and wrong; their moral sense acts as lawgiver and judge within them and either commends or condemns them for what they do. God is absolutely fair. But Paul goes on to show that this breadth of opportunity does not help much. For pagan and Jew alike have failed to keep God's holy law or even their own relative standards, the inner law of conscience. None of us, then, can be reconciled with God on the grounds of our own goodness and sincerity; for no one's goodness and sincerity are perfect—far from it, in fact. Paul's solemn conclusion of that whole passage in the first three chapters of Romans, where he surveys the moral records of religious and pagan worlds alike, is that the whole purpose of the law is "so that every mouth may be stopped, and the whole world may be held accountable to God" (Rom. 3:19). And that is the backdrop against which he sets forth the joyful news that what no one can do for himself, or for anyone else, God has done for all who will trust him, be they religious or pagan by background. He has made it possible for us to be accepted in his beloved Son, Jesus Christ.

Christ died not for our sins only, says the New Testament, "but ... for the sins of the whole world" (1 John 2:2). He died so that men and women of faith in Old Testament days could have their accusing record wiped clean. Of course, Abraham and the others did not know how God would find it possible to accept sinful people like themselves. They just trusted him when he made it clear to them that they were accepted. We, with our greater perspective, know that Abraham was saved because of what God in Christ was going to do for him on that cross of Calvary. It would seem consistent, therefore, with God's gracious activity that those who have not heard of Christ in centuries since Calvary might also wake up on the other side of death to find themselves accepted by God, if they have really repented of their sins and cast themselves upon the mercy of God. For did not Jesus teach us that his heavenly Father is accustomed to giving to everyone who asks and to opening the door to everyone who knocks? The condition of asking, of seeking, of knocking, of repenting in self-abandonment and despair at our own goodness—that is the human side. But God's side has been made plain at the cross. He is prepared to accept any person of any nation at any time into his heavenly kingdom.

It has sometimes been thought that to admit this would be to cut the nerve of missionary endeavor. But this is not the case. Many a missionary has gone to a place where the gospel has never been preached. They have spoken of the love of God for sinners. The response from one or two of his hearers, but by no means all of them, has been to say, "We have been looking for something like this all our lives. We gladly repent and surrender our lives to the God who has so loved us. But, oh, why did you not come and tell us earlier?"

It has sometimes been thought that to admit this "wider hope" is to let us off the hook of deciding for Christ or against him. But nothing could be farther from the truth. The heathen in a pagan land, who repents and believes the first time he hears the gospel, has been searching for years. He is in a very different situation from the careless Western churchgoer who says, "What about all those who have never heard the gospel? Surely all religions lead to God?" in order to avoid commitment of any sort. Such a man is frivolous. He has no excuse for rejecting the Light of the World, Jesus. For the evidence lies open to him in the Scriptures. He is surrounded by Christian believers who know from firsthand experience the truth of what is written in those Scriptures. He is without excuse if he does not follow the lead of the Scriptures and those who have found the truth by coming to Jesus in the surrender of faith and obedience.

Lost

There is one category of people who, the New Testament tells us, will be lost. It is not those who have never heard. It is those who have heard and said no. Such were many of the Pharisees in the time of Jesus. He sadly had to say of them,

> You search the scriptures, because you think that in them you have eternal life; and it is they that bear witness to me; yet you refuse to come to me that you may have life.
>
> John 5:39–40

And when in his second letter to the Christians at Thessalonica Paul speaks of the possibility of hell, he does so in the terrifyingly simple terms of "eternal destruction and exclusion from the presence of the Lord" (2 Thess. 1:9), and he asserts, following his Master, that it awaits those who, having heard the good news of God's rescue, "do not obey the gospel of our Lord Jesus" (v. 8). Let us make sure we do not belong to their number.

8

"Jesus? He's just a myth."

Did Jesus ever live? It's a good question. And in these days of virtual reality, when few people have any grounding in ancient history, it is a question that is often heard. Not only are Christians dismissed as fuddy-duddies in many quarters, but they are fools as well, believing in a Jesus who was probably just a myth, like the classical myths of Mithras and Osiris. The famous philosopher Bertrand Russell said that he regarded the historicity of Jesus as an open question, and plenty of people have written articles and books agreeing with this false premise. I think of J. M. Robertson's attempts to demonstrate the mythical nature of Jesus in his books early in the twentieth century, *Pagan Myths* and *Christianity and Mythology*. I think of an Old Testament scholar and showman, J. M. Allegro, who has gone on record as saying, "Once you break it down to its Semitic sub-stratum you get close to the mystery, fertility cult, which is more significant than we have given it credit for. There is no Jesus, or Joseph, or Mary left. You are dealing with myths."[33] He even proposed that the first Christians got high on "the magic mushroom" (which I discovered does not grow in Israel!) and the whole Christian movement sprang from that.

The heart of the Christian faith is Jesus himself. So at the start of three chapters about him, it is not a bad idea to see if he actually existed.

33. John M. Allegro, *The Dead Sea Scrolls and Christian Myth* (Prometheus Books, 1984).

It has long been Communist policy to assert that he did not exist, and, though Communism is in headlong retreat these days, many of its ideas hang around. At least a quarter of the world's population was subject to this propaganda in the high tide of Communism, and it originated in a fascinating way. In 1842 a German theologian, Bruno Bauer, was deprived of his university chair in Germany because of his extreme heterodox views. This greatly influenced Karl Marx, who, not unnaturally, thought that he had been cruelly wronged by the bourgeois men of religion who dared not allow the shaky foundations of their house of faith to be investigated impartially. Now it was Bauer's view that the historical Jesus was a figment of the imagination of the apostle Mark. He never existed! It is one of the ironies of history (and a judgment on liberal Protestantism) that the vagaries of a heterodox theologian and the sharp reaction of the orthodox should have laid the spiritual foundation for the most powerful atheistic regime the world has ever seen.

But does it actually matter whether Jesus lived or not? Is it not his teaching that is important? After all, Confucianism could survive even if it were proved beyond a shadow of a doubt that Confucius never lived. The same could be said, more or less, for the founders of all the great world religions apart from Christianity and Judaism. History is not important to them: ideas are.

But with Christianity it is entirely different, because Christianity is basically good news about a unique historical person who was born a mere generation before the New Testament authors wrote and was executed under the Roman governor of Judea, Pontius Pilate. He claimed to embody God's final self-disclosure to human beings. He backed up that claim by his matchless teaching, the moral miracle of his blameless life, and his well-substantiated resurrection from the grave.

Such, in brief, is the Christian claim. There is nothing like it in any of the world's other religions. To be sure, it has some features in common with the nature worship of many of the Eastern religions, based as this was on the annual cycle of the birth, maturity, death, and resurrection of the year in its four seasons. The ancient Orient had many variations on this theme in the cults of Dionysus, Attis, Isis and Osiris, Cybele, and Mithras. But with Christianity there was one decisive difference. The Christian claim was attached, as none of these others were, to *a recent historical figure*, one known personally to some of the writers of the New Testament. That is what makes the Christian claim so stark and challenging. It is all about the Jesus of history. Remove him from Christianity and nothing much is left. Once the historicity of Jesus is disproved, the Christian religion will collapse like a pack of cards. For it all depends on this fundamental conviction that God was made manifest in human flesh. And that is a matter not of mythology but of history. So will the Christian claim stand up?

Is the existence of Jesus a myth?

1. Secular evidence about Jesus

You would not expect to find much early non-Christian evidence about the existence of an obscure peasant teacher in an unimportant frontier province of the Roman Empire. Roman historians and men of letters almost all came from the upper classes, who thoroughly disapproved of Eastern religions. Like Juvenal (the great Roman satirist and poet), they felt aggrieved that the Orontes had flowed into the Tiber, bringing a flood of decadent and very un-Roman superstitions in its wake. It would not have been surprising if the birth of Christianity had gone entirely unnoticed by the historians of the period. But this was not the case.

Pliny

The fullest and most interesting account of Christianity from a secular source comes from the pen of Pliny the Younger. He was sent by the emperor Trajan to govern the province of Bithynia in northern Turkey in the year AD 112. We may be grateful for the fact that he was a typical bureaucrat and wrote letters on every conceivable subject to the emperor—no doubt lest he be accused of possessing any personal initiative! One of these letters concerns Christianity. He says that everywhere he went in his province, including villages and country districts, he found Christians. Moreover, their rapid spread had assumed the proportions of a major social problem. The pagan temples had to close down for lack of customers. The sacred festivals had been discontinued, and all demand for sacrificial animals had ceased. Clearly Christianity was very much on the move before the end of the first century, even in so remote a province as this on the edge of the Roman map. Religious disapproval and economic opposition had not succeeded in checking its advance, until Pliny came on the scene and reported to his superior that it now seemed possible, under his capable supervision, to mend the situation!

Those who persisted in their Christianity he executed; such people were obviously rebellious and deserved to die. But he confessed he was much perplexed about the nature of their crime. He had discovered from those who recanted in the face of his persecution that no atrocities were practiced in the Christian assemblies. Their whole guilt lay in this, that they refused to worship the imperial statue and the images of the gods, and they were in the habit of meeting on a fixed day (i.e., Sunday) before it was light, when they sang a hymn to Christ as God (*quasi deo*). They took an oath (perhaps the baptismal promise) not to commit any crimes. Their lives were exemplary. You would not find any fraud, adultery, or theft among them. At their common meal they ate not a murdered infant[34]

---

34. The charge of cannibalism was often made against Christians by the ill-informed, no doubt because believers spoke of "feeding on Christ" in the Holy Communion.

but ordinary food. Pliny was perplexed by the apparent harmlessness of all this, hence his letter to the emperor (*Epistles* 10.96).

Tacitus

Tacitus, a contemporary of Pliny, was the greatest historian of imperial Rome. In his *Annals* (15.44) he tells us how the Christians, hated by the populace for their supposed crimes,[35] were made scapegoats for the Great Fire of AD 64 by the Emperor Nero. "The name Christian," he writes, "comes to them from Christ, who was executed in the reign of Tiberius by the Procurator Pontius Pilate. And the pernicious superstition, suppressed for a while, broke out afresh and spread not only through Judaea, the source of the malady, but even throughout Rome itself, where everything vile comes and is feted."[36]

It is clear that the patrician Tacitus has no sympathy for Christianity, practiced as it was by the lower classes in general and Asians in particular. His evidence, therefore, is all the more valuable. He had good opportunity to get well informed about the origins of Christianity, for in AD 112 he became governor of Asia, where Christians were numerous. Indeed, he referred to them again in a lost book of the *Histories*, of which we have a sentence or two, preserved in a later writer. There he recognizes that the Christian faith began as a sect within Judaism, though it was by his time quite distinct. And he gives the remarkable piece of information that the Roman general Titus hoped, by destroying the temple at Jerusalem in AD 70, to put an end to both Judaism and Christianity, on the theory that if you cut the root, the plant will soon wither!

Writers of the stature of Pliny and Tacitus make the historicity of Jesus certain. But can we go back any farther? Is there any

35. Christian emphasis on "love" for brothers and sisters in Christ was given a sinister interpretation by the pagans: they suspected this secretive movement, the church, to be guilty of incest as well as cannibalism.
36. *The Annals of Tacitus* (Cambridge University Press, 1996).

near-contemporary witness to Jesus among secular writers? It so happens that there is a little.

Earlier testimony

To begin with, there is a statement by the Samaritan historian Thallus, who wrote in Rome about AD 52. His work is lost, but a fragment of it is preserved in the second-century writer Julius Africanus, who tells us, while discussing the darkness that fell when Jesus died on the cross (Mark 15:33): "Thallus, in Book Three of his *History*, explains away the darkness as an eclipse of the sun—unreasonably, as it seems to me."[37] Full marks to Julius Africanus for his objection: you cannot have an eclipse of the sun when the moon is full, as it was at Passover when Jesus died. But the main interest of this quotation lies in showing that the circumstances surrounding the death of Jesus were well known in Rome as early as the middle of the first century, less than twenty years after he died. What is more, they were deemed worthy of inclusion by a secular historian who had set out to write the history of the world!

It is not only the cross of Jesus that was familiar to secular people in the capital by the fifties. So was the story of his resurrection, if we may judge by the probable significance of the following piece of evidence. A remarkable inscription has turned up, belonging to the time of Claudius Caesar, who was emperor from AD 41 to 54. This is the latest the inscription can be dated; many authorities assign it to the reign of Tiberius (AD 14–38). In it he expresses his displeasure at reports he has heard of the removal of bodies of the dead from the tomb, and he gives fair warning that any further tampering with graves will incur nothing short of the death penalty. This inscription was found in Nazareth of all places!

This very sharp threat looks like the imperial reaction to

37. Julius Africanus, *Extant Writings*, XVIII in the *Ante-Nicene Fathers*, ed. Alexander Roberts and James Donaldson (Eerdmans, 1973).

Pilate's report on the crucifixion of Jesus and its sequel, for normally grave robbing was far from a capital offense. It is difficult to imagine that Pilate could have avoided making a report to Rome. After all, Jesus had been executed as a political pretender, and such people were of very special interest to the emperor. Tertullian, a Christian lawyer who lived in the second century, claimed that Pilate's report was still existing in the imperial archives—though this is doubtful, since Tertullian was an advocate prone to exaggeration. Presumably any report from Pilate would have taken the line alluded to in Mathew 28:11–15 that the disciples of Jesus came and stole away the body of Jesus while the soldiers who were supposed to be guarding the tomb slept; hence, naturally enough, the very sharp tone of the emperor.

Claudius was something of an antiquarian and was particularly interested in matters of religion. A papyrus has been discovered in which he takes the Jews of Alexandria to task for rioting with the Greeks, and he is particularly incensed that "certain other Jews" should have sailed down to North Africa from Syria and "fomented a universal plague" in Alexandria among both the Jewish and Greek communities. This has been thought by many competent historians to indicate the arrival of Christianity in Egypt—which in any case must have taken place around that time. If so, it was familiar to Claudius in the first year of his reign (it is hard to date the document any later). In other words, within a decade or less of the crucifixion, the Christian faith was known to the emperor.

In any case, he was bound to take notice of it soon, for it created a problem much nearer home than Alexandria. Suetonius, a court official under Emperor Hadrian and annalist of the imperial house, tells us that Claudius expelled the Jews from Rome, because they were continually rioting "at the instigation of Chrestus" (*impulsore Christo*). The date was AD 49. Two of the people involved in this expulsion order were Aquila and Priscilla, who were Jews by birth but Christians by belief (see Acts 18:2). It appears that Suetonius thought Chrestus (or Christus—the pronunciation was indistinguishable in ancient as in modern Greek) was the leader of one of the factions among the Jews. But clearly the disturbances were caused by the preaching of Christ among the large Jewish community of the capital, particularly as his supporters would urge that he was still very much alive. We have in this slightly muddled report the echo of the tremendous impact made by Christians preaching among the ten thousand or so Jews in Rome, and the acute division in the ghetto caused by the proclamation of a Jesus who was no myth but a very recent and a very disturbing historical figure.

These men, Pliny (AD 61–114), Tacitus (AD 55–118), and Suetonius (AD 69–140), wrote of events that took place a mere thirty years before they were born. Moreover, their official position gave them access to good historical information. The evidence these men give us is more than sufficient to establish the historicity of Jesus, the author of this new faith, who suffered the supreme penalty under Pontius Pilate, while the latter was administering the turbulent province of Judea from AD 26 to 36.

2. Jewish evidence

The most important witness is Josephus. Born in AD 37, his fame rests on two books, the *Jewish War*, published in AD 75, and the *Jewish Antiquities*, published in AD 94. He was one of the Jewish commanders in the disastrous war with Rome and wrote after the destruction of Jerusalem in AD 70 in order to inform the Roman public more accurately about the religion of his fathers and to reestablish some credit for Judaism in their minds. These two apologetic works would naturally keep to the minimum any material that would irritate his Roman readers. We find in his pages many of the figures familiar from the New Testament: Pilate, the Herods, Caiaphas, Quirinius, Felix, Festus, and many others.

Twice Josephus refers to Jesus. Once he speaks of James, "the brother of Jesus who was called Christ." And once he gives an extended reference to Jesus, as follows:

> And there arose about this time [i.e., Pilate's time, AD 26–36] Jesus, a wise man, if indeed we should call him a man; for he was a doer of marvelous deeds, a teacher of men who receive the truth with pleasure. He won over many Jews, and also many Greeks. This man was the Christ. And when Pilate had condemned him to the cross at the instigation of our own leaders, those who loved him from the first did not cease. For he appeared to them on the third day alive again, as the holy prophets had predicted and said many other wonderful things about him. And even now the race of Christians, so called after him, has not disappeared.
>
> *(Antiquities* 18.3.3) [38]

This is, of course, a most surprising testimony to find in the pages of one who was not a Christian; accordingly, strenuous scholarly attempts have been made to impugn its authenticity. However, it has as good an attestation as anything else in Josephus; it is included in all the manuscripts. We know that the fourth-century historian Eusebius had it in his copy of Josephus; he quotes it twice. No doubt some of the Josephus passage is sarcastic. "If indeed we should call him a man" may allude to reports of his divine claims, just as the passage about the resurrection may be reflecting what the Christians maintained. "He was the Christ" may refer to the charge affixed to his cross and may also reflect Josephus's own disillusion with Jewish attempts to rebel against Rome; he knew Jesus had confessed before Caiaphas that he was the Messiah (or Christ)—and he knew what had resulted. The Christ or Messiah was crucified, while the corrupt priesthood stayed in charge under Roman overlords. As Professor Carsten Thiede put it,

---

38. Flavius Josephus, *Antiquities of the Jews,* Book XVIII, public domain online at http://www.ccel.org/j/josephus/JOSEPHUS.HTM.

"The Messiah came, and the Messiah went, destroyed by the Romans. All messianic hope had been in vain.... The message of Josephus to his fellow Jews is stark: do not revolt against the Romans and forget about the Messiah. We had him and he failed."[39]

Be that as it may, we have in Josephus an early, powerful, and independent testimony to the historical reality of Jesus of Nazareth. The stories about Jesus were no myth. They were so circumstantial and so well attested that they even found a place in this apologetic work of the Jewish Josephus; and he had the strongest possible reason for keeping quiet about anything so inconvenient to his theme.

There is a good deal of other evidence—Jewish, archaeological, and Christian. But I think enough has been said to show that Jesus was no myth. He was the flesh-and-blood figure whose coming split all history in two.

Is the divinity of Jesus a myth?

It is one thing to show that Jesus was a historical figure but quite another to go along with the Christian claim that he was divine. Might he not just have been a remarkable man around whom myths of divinity began to gather? After all, there were plenty of people in the ancient world, such as Alexander the Great, who laid claim to divine parentage. As the Christian faith began to emerge in the secular world, where such stories were fairly common, is it not natural that Jesus too simply had to be proclaimed as divine if he was to compete?

Such views were written up by a group of scholars some years ago in a book called *The Myth of God Incarnate*. One of them attributes belief in the deity of Jesus to the supposed influence of Simon Magus on the church. Others speak of the power of hysteria within a small community. All divinity language was,

39. Carsten Peter Thiede in personal correspondence with the author.

at most, poetic and later hardened into prose. They concluded
that we simply cannot believe it.

The testimony of the New Testament

Well, the New Testament writers were not poetic about it at all.
They were all of one very definite mind—namely, that God had
invaded this world in the person of Jesus Christ. Listen to what
Paul, in probably his earliest letter, wrote to the Thessalonians
in AD 50. He reminded them how they had "turned to God
from idols, to serve a living and true God, and to wait for his
Son from heaven, whom he raised from the dead, Jesus who
delivers us from the wrath to come" (1 Thess. 1:10). To the
Corinthians he writes some three years later:

> There is one God, the Father, from whom are all things and for
> whom we exist, and one Lord, Jesus Christ, through whom are all
> things and through whom we exist.
>
> 1 Corinthians 8:6

In his second letter to Corinth, Paul speaks of "the light of the
gospel of the glory of Christ, who is the image of God" (4:4 NIV).

The New Testament writers are just as clear on the divinity of
Jesus. Mark heads his Gospel, "The beginning of the gospel
of Jesus Christ, the Son of God" (Mark 1:1). Matthew is keen to
explain why, before his birth, he is to be called Jesus. The name
means "God to the rescue." He is to have that name because
"he will save his people from their sins" (Matt. 1:21). In the Old
Testament that was going to be God's job (see Ps. 130:8). But
what was God's job Jesus fulfills. The apostle John is the most
explicit of them all. "The Word" is his philosophical term for
Jesus in his first chapter. The Word was in the beginning with
God. The Word is the principle of life. The Word is the agent in
creation. The Word is the light of the world. In short, the Word
is God. And then John says what no Greek philosopher, no
Hebrew prophet would ever have dared to say about anyone—
that this Word became flesh and dwelt among us. John

concludes, in his amazing first chapter, "no one has ever seen God ... but God the One and Only, who is at the Father's side [as the best manuscripts read], has made him known" (John 1:18 NIV).

Wherever you look in the New Testament, you find this same confident assurance about the divinity of Jesus. One of the oldest passages in the Gospels, recorded both by Matthew and Luke, gives us these words of Jesus:

> All things have been delivered to me by my Father; and no one knows the Son except the Father, and no one knows the Father except the Son and any one to whom the Son chooses to reveal him.
>
> Matthew 11:27; see also Luke 10:22

Notice how Jesus claims a unique relationship with the Father. He alone knows the Father. He alone can introduce people to the Father. He is the one through whom God the Father makes himself known.

Finally, glance at the opening words of the Epistle to the Hebrews, written by some unknown Christian about AD 67.

> In many and various ways God spoke of old to our fathers by the prophets; but in these last days he has spoken to us by a Son, whom he appointed the heir of all things, through whom also he created the world. He reflects the glory of God and bears the very stamp of his nature, upholding the universe by his word of power.
>
> Hebrews 1:1–3

All the New Testament writers had come to the conclusion that in a unique personal way "God was in Christ." This was no exaggeration, no hyperbole, no mythological language or poetic license. They meant it to be taken with the utmost seriousness. They believed in the truth of God incarnate.

What gave the first Christians this conviction about Jesus?

Was there any precedent for the astonishing claim of these first Christians? Was there something in their culture that made it comparatively easy for them to believe in the divinity of Jesus?

Were there any such ideas in the Greek world? Yes, indeed. At first sight there are lots of parallels to the incarnation, death, and resurrection of Jesus in the old myths about Apollo and Asclepius, Hercules and Tammuz. What if Jesus was called Lord by his followers? So was Serapis. What if he was said to have been born of a virgin? So were half the members of the pantheon. What if he was supposed to have ascended to heaven? So was Hercules, and so were practically all the Roman emperors (it all began when someone claimed they had seen a new star arise from Julius Caesar's funeral pyre!). What was so special, then, about Jesus?

The really special thing was this: nobody had ever attributed divinity and a virgin birth, resurrection, and ascension to a historical person whom lots of people knew. And certainly nobody ever claimed that the one and only God, the Creator and the Judge of the whole earth, had embodied himself in Apollo, Hercules, Augustus, and the rest. Folk like Apollo were mythical figures whom nobody in their right mind believed in. Folk like Hercules, born of the amours of Zeus with mortal women, were equally imaginary. As for the ruler cult that divinized "Rome and Augustus," it was just a convenient tool for controlling the empire and nobody took it seriously. Seneca poked fun at it in his *Pumpkinification of Claudius* in the fifties, and as the Emperor Vespasian exclaimed when he lay dying in the seventies, "Oh dear, I think I am becoming a god!" It is very difficult to see the Christian conviction springing from such roots. But no better ones have been suggested. To be sure, a man called Wilhelm Bousset published an influential book a century ago, entitled *Kyrios Christos*, which argued that the idea of calling Jesus Lord arose on pagan Greek soil where, as the apostle Paul acknowledged, there were "many lords." There is only one problem with that. The title did not originate on pagan soil at all but on Jewish! We have its original Aramaic in the formula *"Maranatha"* (see 1 Cor. 16:22). Depending on how you divide the word up, it means either "Our Lord has come" or the invocation "O our Lord, come!" It either attests the incarnation or the future coming in glory of Jesus. And it shows that Jesus was addressed as *"Mar,"* one of the words for God, in the earliest Aramaic-speaking community.

Well, if the idea did not come from the Hellenistic world into which Christianity soon spread, did they get it from their Jewish background? It does not look likely because the Jews were such fanatical monotheists. So much so that they would not take the sacred name of God (YHWH) upon their lips. Indeed, at Qumran, washbasins were found in the library where the Dead Sea Scrolls were written to allow for a ceremonial washing of the hands whenever the divine name was written down! In other words, if you had looked the whole world over for a more stony or improbable soil in which to plant the idea of a divine incarnation, you could not have done better than Israel! They refused to have any representation of God whatsoever, be it in pictures, statues, or any other art form. The Romans who conquered them could never get over the fact that when their general Pompey burst into the Holy of Holies in the temple at Jerusalem he found no statue there! So the Jews became known in Roman circles as atheists. It was in this background, and no other, that the conviction arose that God had incarnated himself in human flesh. The Christians certainly did not get the idea from Judaism.

Why on earth, then, did these early Christians believe in the deity of Jesus, if there are no adequate parallels either in their Jewish background or in Greek paganism? The answer is obvious. The idea that God could possibly reveal himself in a human being was initially utterly alien to the early Christians, but their companionship with Jesus of Nazareth persuaded them that he had done so. Jesus could not be confined to the category of the human.

Reluctantly, slowly, these Jewish monotheists came to accept that Jesus must be more than man. Such was their trembling speculation after living alongside him for two or three years (see Matt. 16:16, for instance). But after the resurrection the conviction became unshakeable (see Rom. 1:4, for instance). They were driven to it inexorably as they reflected on his amazing teaching, his sinless moral life, his astounding claims, his staggering miracles, his fulfillment of prophecy, his sacrificial cross, and his glorious resurrection. You could persecute these first Christians, torture them, throw them to the lions—and all this happened. No matter what, you could not shatter their conviction that the deity of Jesus was no myth but one of the most solid facts in all history.

9

"Jesus was just a good man."

Ours is a questioning generation. We won't take anything on authority, and if an opinion is old, it is probably wrong! We want instant truth, instant relevance. Old dogmas, such as the church's view that Jesus of Nazareth was divine, simply don't turn us on anymore. And yet we remain fascinated by Jesus. Books about him continue to pour from the presses despite the soaring cost of paper and printing. Films and rock operas about him are box-office successes. He certainly has not lost his appeal. But we aren't quite sure what to make of him. He seems somehow different from other people.

Let's get back to the New Testament documents and look a bit closer at that difference—and then see whether the easy solution, "Jesus was just a good man," will carry conviction or not.

1. His character was different

Different from anyone who ever lived. That character has dominated the world in the two thousand years since he walked the narrow streets of Nazareth. To be sure, Mohammed has had a profound influence, and so has Socrates. But nothing like Jesus. Jesus has captured the heart and mind and allegiance of peasant and king, of intellectual and illiterate the world over, all down the centuries. It makes no difference whether you go to the Naga tribesmen in the hill country of India, or the warlike Masai in Kenya, black and white in Southern Africa, the United States, the people of Fiji and of Finland, of

Singapore and Sevastopol. Everywhere there are Christians. Wherever the message of this man Jesus has been proclaimed, some people of every tribe and culture and background and intellect have turned from their own ways to follow him. This has brought opposition, often persecution. It has meant self-sacrifice and ostracism. But that has not stopped people succumbing to the spell of Jesus.

Where do you find, in the whole history of humanity, a character that has dominated and appealed to men and women of every generation and type, and in so doing has transformed them for the better? Nowhere but in Jesus. That one solitary life is without parallel. Do you know that anonymous piece entitled "One Solitary Life"? Here it is:

> He was born in an obscure village, the child of a peasant woman.
>
> He grew up in still another village, where he worked in a carpenter's shop till he was thirty. Then for three years he was an itinerant preacher.
>
> He never wrote a book. He never held an office. He never had a family or owned a house. He didn't go to college. He never visited a big city. He never traveled two hundred miles from the place where he was born. He did none of the things one usually associates with greatness.
>
> He had no credentials but himself.
>
> He was only thirty-three when the tide of public opinion turned against him. His friends ran away. He was turned over to his enemies and went through the mockery of a trial. He was nailed to a cross between two thieves. While he was dying, his executioners gambled for his clothing, the only property he had on earth. When he was dead he was laid in a borrowed grave through the pity of a friend.
>
> Twenty centuries have come and gone, and today he is the central figure of the human race and the leader of mankind's progress. All the armies that ever marched, all the navies that ever sailed, all the parliaments that ever sat, all the kings that ever reigned, put together, have not affected the life of man on this earth as much as that ONE SOLITARY LIFE.

If Jesus was just a good person, I wonder what it was that made his life so different. Those who say he was just an ordinary individual find this difficult to answer. For example, followers of today's New Age movement might try to make him fit their view of the world by saying that he simply reached a high plane of consciousness, a rarefied level of reality. And yet this explanation doesn't fit. This person is like no other political, moral, or spiritual leader the world has ever seen. No guru or channel comes anywhere near Jesus. There is, you see, something different about him.

2. His teaching was different

Nobody ever taught like this. That was the conclusion of the soldiers sent to arrest him. The apostle John tells us that when the Pharisees asked them why they had not obeyed orders, they replied, "No man ever spoke like this man!" (John 7:46). He taught them, says the earliest evangelist, as one who had authority, and not like the teachers of the day. These men would prop up their opinions by endless references to teachers before them who had held the same view—rather like the acres of footnotes in modern scholarly books about God. Jesus prefaced his teaching with the remarkable formula, unknown in all literature, "Truly, truly I say to you." Who was this "I" who spoke with such authority? Who was this person who spoke so much about the kingdom of God and calmly announced that he was bringing it in? "The Law and the Prophets were proclaimed until John," he once said. "Since that time, the good news of the kingdom of God is being preached" (Luke 16:16 NIV). In other words, his forerunner, John the Baptist, marked the end of the old era. Jesus inaugurated the new. This accounts for the note of urgency that runs through those remarkable parables of his. The planter who has been sowing and tending his seed now has to harvest the crop: if he lets the moment pass, the crop is lost. The pearl fancier who finds the best pearl he has ever seen, or the farmer who turns up a bag of buried treasure in a field—for both, zero hour has arrived; they must go for it even if it means losing everything. The generous householder has spread his banquet and invited all and sundry; to make excuses at this juncture, to refuse the invitation would be disastrous—it would mean final exclusion from the party. No wonder the whole countryside was agog at teaching like this. There was nothing comparable in the religious history of the world.

You only had to compare Jesus's teaching with the Old Testament to get the message. Now, don't get me wrong. Jesus took the Old Testament as his Bible. He believed that it was inspired by God, and was therefore decisive both for himself and his hearers. But still he can contrast his teaching with it, not as black against white but as fulfillment of promise. "I have not come to abolish the law and the prophets, but to fulfill them," he claimed (see Matt. 5:17). And he proceeded to show what he meant. "Your goodness has to be better than that of the religious leaders," he maintained (see Matt. 5:20)—and explained that many religious people make a show of their piety in order to impress others; they give so as to be praised by others; and they pray so as to be seen by others. Secret prayer, unseen generosity, unostentatious religion is the order of the day for the follower of Jesus.

Or take the matter of murder.

> You have heard that it was said to the men of old, "You shall not kill; and whoever kills shall be liable to judgment." But I say to you that every one who is angry with his brother shall be liable to judgment.
>
> Matthew 5:21–22

Jesus is not abolishing the Old Testament law of manslaughter. He is fulfilling the principle behind it, for he is showing how God hates the evil thought of uncontrolled fury no less than the bitter outcome of murder. Again, he takes the famous maxim from the Old Testament, "An eye for an eye and a tooth for a tooth" and adds, "But I say to you, Do not resist one who is evil" (Matt. 5:38). Is he repudiating the Old Testament teaching? Not at all. He perceives the principle that lay behind it (that of limiting revenge by the equivalent of the wrong done) and fulfills that principle by allowing love to banish revenge altogether.

This matter of love was hard enough to fulfill, even for the friends you liked. So the Old Testament had said, "You shall love your neighbor," and to it the scribes had enthusiastically added what the Old Testament did not add, "and hate your enemy"! To this Jesus brings an undreamed-of fulfillment, a new thing in the history of thought, an ethic that is the most difficult and the most powerful in today's world, as it was then:

> But I say to you, Love your enemies, and pray for those who perse-
> cute you, so that you may be sons of your Father who is in heaven.
> Matthew 5:44

If you want more of this, turn to the Sermon on the Mount in Matthew chapters 5–7. But the point is clear enough. Though Jesus built on God's revelation in the Old Testament, he taught a fulfillment of what had been foreshadowed there, which was breathtakingly new, completely lucid, intensely profound, and as relevant now as it was then.

Now I ask you: where can you find anything in the teaching of Jesus that does not strike you as truth? How do you account for the fact that no ethical advances, no teaching of how people should behave toward each other has emerged in the centuries since then that represents any advance on Jesus? Where did the man get this fantastic teaching from? He had an answer: "My teaching is not mine, but his who sent me" (John 7:16). Could he be right? Did he come from God? Could this account at one fell swoop for his authority, his simplicity, his depth, his worldwide appeal? If you reply, "Of course not; he was just a very impressive teacher," I want to ask you a question or two.

Why did he strike contemporaries and subsequent generations as so utterly different from other teachers? How is it that
he got all this learning without having been to college? How is
it that, unlike other great teachers such as Socrates and
Mohammed, his teaching fits all people everywhere? How is it
that nobody has dreamed up any moral advances since his
teaching? What was there in his heredity and his environment
to account for this unique teacher and the remarkable fact that
no greater has ever looked like emerging? Yes, there was
something different about this teacher. Perhaps it was not so
strange when he took over the old Jewish saying, "When two or
three busy themselves over the law of God, the glory of God
shines upon them," and replaced it with, "Where two or three
are gathered in my name, there am I in the midst of them"
(Matt. 18:20). Perhaps he *was* different.

3. His behavior was different

Time and time again he told doubters not to believe him unless
his behavior bore him out. His works, as he sometimes called
them, had to match his words. And they did. Exactly. How
sublime to be able to tell the story of the shepherd who goes
out at night and braves danger to seek one lost sheep—and
continues to look until he finds it. But more sublime still is to
go and live it out by loving a Simon Peter, even when he denied
knowing him and deserted him in his moment of greatest
need. It is marvelous to find Jesus talking of the love his Father
has for all people irrespective of their merits; love that, like the
rain and sunshine, falls on all alike. It is even more marvelous
to give the best portion at a supper party to the man you know
is just about to betray you, and then to kiss him on the cheek as
you do so! It is one thing to say, "Blessed are the poor," and
quite another to be happy in poverty, as Jesus was. One thing to
say, "Bless your enemies," and quite another matter to cry,
"Father, forgive them" as cruel soldiers nail your bleeding body

to a cross. But that is the way Jesus behaved. His actions matched his teaching.

That is something that has never been equaled. Socrates, Plato, Moses, Confucius, and, in our own day, Martin Luther King, Pope John, Bob Geldof, Mother Teresa, and Billy Graham taught wonderful things and people have hung on their words. But never did any of these great leaders actually manage to carry out all they taught. In all of them there has been consciousness of failure. Indeed, this is one of the surest marks of greatness—to recognize that one's objective exceeds one's reach, and the goal lies beyond the achievement. And growth in greatness always carries with it growth in humility. Talk to any truly great individuals, and they will tell you how ashamed they are of their failures and mistakes. The most famous saints are always most conscious of wrong within.

But Jesus was different. He taught the highest standards that any teacher has formulated, and he kept them. He really did. There is remarkable unanimity on this matter. It is interesting to note how united the opposition to Jesus is about his innocence. Three times in the account of the trial before Pilate, the governor pronounces him innocent. Pilate's wife sends a message to the courtroom to the same effect. The Jewish leaders cannot find an accusation that will stick, and so they have to get him to incriminate himself by admitting to be the Messiah. Even the traitor Judas confesses that he has betrayed innocent blood. Even one of the thieves crucified with him recognized that he had done nothing wrong. Even the man in charge of the crucifixion was driven to exclaim, "This man was innocent." Quite an impressive bunch of testimonies from the opposition. Jesus was different.

Perhaps still more impressive is the testimony of his friends. The more we know someone, the less inclined we are to entertain any exaggerated claim on their behalf; we know them too well. But not in Jesus's case. The apostle John knew him intimately. Yet he could call Jesus "the true Light that gives light to every man" (John 1:9 NIV) and could assert, "If we say that we have no sin, we deceive ourselves" (1 John 1:8) but "in him there is no sin" (1 John 3:5). Peter could call him "the just one" in contrast to us "the unjust" (see 1 Pet. 3:18), and he could be so overcome by the quality of Jesus's life that he fell at his feet on one occasion and asked him to depart from a sinner like himself. Paul calls Jesus "the sinless one"; the writer to the Hebrews spoke of him as just the one we need, "holy, blameless, unstained, separated from sinners" (Heb. 7:26). In short, every strand of the New Testament, written as it was by those who knew Jesus or knew of him well, is quite clear on this matter: his life was perfect. It was a moral miracle. His life was different from other men's and showed theirs up.

This is precisely what we seem to find in Jesus's own allusions to his behavior. We never find him having to apologize. We never find him having to admit he was wrong. And this from the one who was so shrewd in spotting hypocrisy in others! There are several occasions when we are given the substance of his prayers, but never once do they betray any shadow of consciousness of guilt. He does tell us to pray, "Forgive us our trespasses," but significantly he does not seem to need to do so himself. Fascinating. Unique. Here is a person of the most refined spiritual insight, who can say of his heavenly Father, "I always do what is pleasing to him" (John 8:29). Here is a person who can turn to an angry crowd, furious because he was claiming that he was one with God, and with childlike innocence can ask them, "Which of you convicts me of sin?" (John 8:46). I do not know which is the more remarkable: that he could ask such a question—or that the crowd could not give an answer!

Whichever way you look at it, that life was unique. He alone, of all the people known to history, has come down to us with a clean sheet. No mud slung at him has stuck. His behavior was blameless. What other person has behaved like that? Even for one day? OK, then, will it do simply to say, "Jesus was no more than a fine teacher"? Isn't that a very shallow assumption, in the light of a life that was so staggeringly different?

4. His abilities were different

You cannot disentangle Jesus from miracles. Scholars in the last century spent endless ingenuity on the quest of a non-miraculous Jesus. In the end, it was an acknowledged failure. Because every strand in the evidence about Jesus shows him as different from other people; through him God acted in a way impossible to understand on the assumption that he was just a good man. The miracles begin at his birth: he was God's Son, according to Mark; God's Word and agent in creation, according to John; the full repository of the Godhead, according to Paul (while, nevertheless, being "born of a woman"); the one who came into the world without the agency of a human father, according to Matthew and Luke. The miracles continue in his ministry: miracles of healing, of exorcism; nature miracles (such as the feeding of the multitude from a handful of loaves and his walking on the sea in a storm); and, supremely, his raising from the dead of Lazarus, the widow of Nain's son, and Jairus's daughter. Last of all came the greatest of all miracles, his own resurrection from the grave—not just to a further span of life but to a new quality of life, over which death has no power.

Such is the testimony of the New Testament: a Jesus who was different, in view of the powers at his command. In the first three Gospels, these miracles are actually called "acts of power" in the original Greek. But John's Gospel shows the true significance of the miracles when he calls them "signs." Signs of who Jesus is. Signs of what he can do for men and women. The one who fed a multitude can feed the hungry soul. The one who opened blind eyes can do the same for those blinded by pride and prejudice. The one who raised the dead can bring new life to someone who is dead spiritually and morally. The miracles were never done for selfish purposes, never to show off. They were evoked by Jesus's compassion for human need, and they were intended both to show that the long-awaited messianic kingdom had begun and also that Jesus was the liberator who could loose the various chains of human beings. It is fashionable to laugh at the miracles. Such things could not happen. But why not? The laws of nature do not forbid them. A "law of nature" is simply the name we give to a series of observed uniformities: this is the way things happen. But if a contrary instance is well attested, scientists will widen their so-called "law" to embrace both the uniformities and the exception to the rule. In the case of Jesus, there is lots of strong contemporary evidence that he was the exception to the rule. If he was just a good man, that would be astonishing, perhaps meaningless. If he was different, if he was in some way God himself, coming to disclose himself to us within the limitations of human form—then perhaps it is neither so incredible nor so meaningless that he should perform miracles.

At all events the evidence is overwhelming, and it is not all contained within the pages of the New Testament. You will find the earliest Christian apologist, a man called Quadratus, writing very early in the second century:

> But the works of our Savior were always present (for they were genuine); namely those who were healed, those who rose from the dead. They were not only seen in the act of being healed or raised, but they remained always present. And not merely when the Savior was on earth, but after his departure as well. They lived on for a considerable time, so much so that some of them have survived even to our own day.[40]

I find it intriguing that this, the only passage of Quadratus to have survived, should be devoted to drawing out the implications and establishing the truth of the miracles. It shows how

40. See http://www.earlychristianwritings.com/text/quadratus.html.

confidently the early Christians could look to the miracles of Jesus as a pointer to his being more than a man, to his being different.

But there are traces of his miracles in Roman and Jewish sources as well. Justin Martyr, writing his *Apology* about AD 150, can say with casual confidence, "That he performed these miracles you may easily satisfy yourself from the *Acts* of Pontius Pilate." It was the same with the Jews. We find them in the Gospels unable to deny the miracles of Jesus but taking the only way out—attributing them to the devil. In the Acts of the Apostles, we find Jews attempting to use the name of Jesus as a potent spell in exorcism; later on this continued, so much so that the writers in the *Mishnah* (Jewish law code) have to forbid Jews to heal in the name of Jesus! And the Tractate *Sanhedrin* tells that Jesus "was hanged on the eve of the Passover because he practiced sorcery and led Israel astray"—a plain reference to his miracles.

Clearly, this Jesus was not just like the rest of us. He had abilities that marked him as different.

5. His fulfillment of Scripture was different

Strikingly different. It hit the first disciples between the eyes. So much so that they found themselves writing like this: "This was done in order to fulfill the words of the prophet Isaiah . . ." and the like. It is a recurring theme in the New Testament. Now this is very remarkable. The first followers of Jesus, being Jews, had the highest reverence for the Scriptures of the Old Testament. Yet there were manifestly incomplete sides to them. Those Scriptures spoke of a day when God would judge the earth. They spoke of a king of David's stock whose dominion would be endless. They spoke of all the families of the world being blessed in Abraham, the man of faith who had started the nation of Israel. They spoke of one like a Son of Man coming to the Ancient of Days and receiving a kingdom that would never be destroyed, together with power, glory, and judgment. They spoke of a prophet like Moses arising among the people, whose teaching would be unparalleled. They spoke of a servant of the Lord whose suffering would be intense and whose death would carry away the sins of the people. They spoke of a Son of God whose character would measure up to that of his Father. This Coming One would fulfill the role of prophet, of priest, and of king forever. He would be born of David's lineage, but of a humble, despised family. His birthplace would be Bethlehem. He would both restore the fallen in Israel and be a light to the Gentiles. He would be despised and rejected by the very people he came to rescue from their self-centeredness. He would die among criminals, and his tomb would be supplied by a rich man. But that would not be the end of him. He would live again, and the Lord's program would prosper in his hand. When he saw all that would be accomplished by the anguish of his soul, he would be satisfied. For he would have forged a new agreement between God and man by his death; indeed, his death would open up the possibility of ordinary men and women having the Spirit of God come and take up residence within their lives.

All of this came true with Jesus. Not some of it: all of it. There is no example in the literature of the whole world where the prophecies made centuries beforehand in a holy book were fulfilled in a historical person in this way. It amazed his followers, but it convinced them. They came to see in him, the humble carpenter of Nazareth, the fulfillment of these ancient prophecies. He was born in Bethlehem of David's stock. His teaching showed him to be the prophet like Moses. He was the Suffering Servant of the Lord, whose anguish on the cross brought pardon for all who would believe, as Abraham had believed. He was the one who would restore the fortunes of Israel and open up the way of faith to the Gentiles. He had established this new covenant between God and man, sealing it with his blood. His death had made the ultimate sacrifice, and no priesthood was ever to be needed again—for he had once and for all reconciled men and women to God by his own self-offering. His kingly rule would be forever—veiled now, but apparent when he came to judge. His Spirit was already at work in the transformed lives of the disciples.

In the centuries that followed, this argument from prophecy had an enormous impact. Many distinguished pagans were won to faith in Jesus by the way he fulfilled the prophecies made in these writings of an Old Testament, which seemed so much older and so much nobler than their own writings of Homer and Plato. And many still are. As Professor Moule, one of the leading New Testament scholars in England, put it:

> The notion of the "fulfilment" of Scripture in a single individual, a figure of recent history, and he a condemned and disgraced criminal, who claimed to be the coping stone of the whole structure, and the goal of God's whole design, was new. And it was the Christian community which first related together, round a single focus, the scattered and largely disconnected images of Israel's hope.[41]

That figure *was* different.

So different that we find the New Testament writers attributing to him titles and activities reserved for God himself in the Old Testament. For instance, in Isaiah (41:4; 44:6; 48:12) God calls himself "the first and the last," but in the New Testament this title is applied to Jesus (see Rev. 1:8; 2:8; 22:13). "I am" is the special name of God ("Yahweh," usually known as "Jehovah") and to the Jews it is too sacred to be pronounced, so they use the word "Adonai" ("Lord") as a substitute. But we find claims to be the "I am" coming on the lips of Jesus, notably the fantastic claim of John 8:58, "before Abraham was, I am." So much so that when asked at a crucial stage in his trial whether he was the Messiah, Jesus replied,

41. C. F. D. Moule, *The Phenomenon of the New Testament* (SCM, 1967).

I am; and you will see the Son of man seated at the right hand of
Power, and coming with the clouds of heaven.

Mark 14:62

This produced a savage reaction in the high priest and his
colleagues because it was seen to be a claim to personal deity on
the part of Jesus.

Again, who is it in the Old Testament who is the shepherd of
his people? God, of course. "The LORD is my shepherd" begins
that most famous Psalm 23. But Jesus calmly uses the title
of himself, "I am the good shepherd" (John 10:14); and
other New Testament writers such as Peter and the author of
Hebrews speak of him as "the chief shepherd" and "the great
shepherd." They had gotten the message.

Perhaps the most remarkable function of God in the Old
Testament was to create the world. "In the beginning, God
created the heaven and the earth" is, after all, the opening
sentence of the whole Bible. But listen to Paul: "In him [Christ]
all things were created, in heaven and on earth ... all things
were created through him and for him" (Col. 1:16). And listen
to John: "He was in the beginning with God; all things were
made through him, and without him was not anything made
that was made" (John 1:2–3).

Clearly, this man was different. No good man fulfilled all the
strands of ancient Scriptures, themselves penned over a thousand years, as this man did. Perhaps his contemporaries were
right in believing he was one with God.

6. His claims were different

If you have read the Gospels, you may well have been struck
by a remarkable contrast. On the one hand, Jesus is a humble,
self-forgetful figure, healing the sick, teaching the people,
befriending the outcast. He is no academic theologian but
a carpenter with calloused hands, whose words are full of

hardheaded wisdom and earthy illustrations. He has no money, no settled home, no vote, no rights. On the other hand, he makes the most fantastic claims, and many of them are almost casual, offhand remarks. For example, he takes it for granted that he is entitled to man's worship, the worship due to God alone. When Peter falls at his feet in adoration after a fishing expedition and says, "Depart from me, for I am a sinful man, O Lord" (Luke 5:8), Jesus does nothing to stop him. When Thomas falls at his feet after the resurrection and exclaims, "My Lord and my God!" (John 20:28), Jesus does not rebuke him—except for needing the evidence of his eyes to come to that conclusion. No good person would do that. Indeed, we have examples in the New Testament of two good men, Peter and Paul, who found themselves being worshipped by ignorant pagans, and they reacted violently against it, telling them to worship God alone. Jesus seems to have accepted such worship as his due.

Watch him deal with a woman accused of adultery (see John 8:1–11) or a man sick with paralysis (see Mark 2:1–12). In both instances, Jesus forgave their sins, and in the case of the paralytic, he gave a visual demonstration of the fact— the man got up at Jesus's command and walked! Now what are we to make of a claim like that? The Pharisees knew very well what to make of it. "Who is this that forgives sins?" they asked. "There is one who forgives sins, God." That is precisely the point. Jesus was laying implicit claim to do what God does, to forgive people their sins. Indeed, when Mary is told that her baby must be called Jesus, the explanation of the name is brought out like this: "for he will save his people from their sins" (Matt. 1:21). In the Old Testament (Ps. 130:8), the authority to forgive sins is solely, and naturally, said to belong to God alone. Here, right at the start of his life, Jesus takes on the job. The implication is obvious. In Jesus we meet someone who is *different*.

What are we to make of this? C. S. Lewis puts the challenge with his customary force.

There is no halfway house, and there is no parallel in other religions. If you had gone to Buddha and asked him: "Are you the son of Bramah?" he would have said, "My son, you are still in the vale of illusion." If you had gone to Socrates and asked, "Are you Zeus?" he would have laughed at you. If you had gone to Mohammed and asked, "Are you Allah?" he would first have rent his clothes and then cut off your head. If you had asked Confucius, "Are you heaven?" I think he would probably have replied, "Remarks which are not in accordance with nature are in bad taste."[42]

This man was different. He was not merely a great teacher.

Listen to Lewis once again:

> The things he says are very different from what any other teacher has said. Others say, "This is the truth about the universe. This is the way you ought to go." But he says, "I am the Truth and the Way and the Life." He says, "No man can reach absolute reality, except through me. Try to retain your own life and you will inevitably be ruined. Give yourself away and you will be saved." He says, "If you are ashamed of me, if, when you hear my call, you turn the other way, I will look the other way when I come again as God without disguise. If anything whatever is keeping you from God and from me, whatever it is, throw it away. If it is your eye, pull it out. If it is your hand, cut it off. If you put yourself first you will be last. Come to me, everyone who is carrying a heavy load, and I will set that right. Your sins, all of them, are wiped out. I can do that. I am Re-birth, I am Life. Eat me, drink me, I am your food. And finally, do not be afraid, I have overcome the whole universe." That is the issue.[43]

Yes, that is the issue. What are you going to make of it? In the light of his character and teaching, his behavior and miracles, his fulfillment of prophecy and his astonishing claims, what are you going to say? He backed the whole thing up with a

42. C. S. Lewis, *God in the Dock: Essays on Theology and Ethics* (Eerdmans, 1970).
43. Ibid.

death such as the world has never seen and, unlike any other person before or since, a resurrection from the grave. (I shall deal with his cross in chapter 11 and his resurrection in chapter 12.) It was the way he died and the way he rose that supremely convinced the first disciples that the man Jesus was nothing less than God. He "was declared with power to be the Son of God by his resurrection from the dead," wrote Saul of Tarsus (Rom. 1:4 NIV), who was once such a formidable opponent of the Christian faith but was now convinced that Jesus's claims were true.

Evidence

Take a long, hard look at the evidence I have brought before you in this chapter. Read diligently any one of the Gospels with an open mind. And then if you still say, "Jesus was just a good man," I shall say, "You can't be serious!" That is the one thing he cannot be. That is the one thing the people on the spot never thought of calling him. They were terrified of him; they believed him; or they hounded him to death. But nobody patronizingly said of him, "What a splendid preacher we had in the synagogue last Sabbath. You must come along and hear him some time." Jesus does not present himself to us as the best example of the human race, for our edification. He comes to us from beyond the human race as God himself, hastening to our rescue. He expects of us, indeed demands of us, not our admiration but our allegiance, not our patronage but our hearts. He has the rights of God Almighty over us. And he can make all the difference of God Almighty within us, once we allow room for him in the lives he has given us. The question is, Shall we let him?

10

"I do my best.
No one can do more."

Christianity is a rescue religion. That is why it is so unpopular. It goes to the heart of human nature and makes a radical difference. But when men and women pause from the rat race for a moment to take a long cool look at themselves in the light of their own standards, they tend to come up with two main attitudes. One takes a rosy view of human nature and says in effect, "I do my best. That ought to be good enough for whatever God there may be. I'll be okay." The other is more pessimistic and says, "I've made a mess of things. Nothing can change the past." We'll look at them in turn: the optimist in this chapter and the pessimist in the next. They are closely connected, in actual fact. They are two opposite reactions to the problem of guilt.

The problem of guilt

However hard-boiled you are, there are times when you feel dirty, rotten, guilty. It may nag away at you for years or it may just hit you once in a while, as it comes through in Roger McGough's poem "Come Close and Sleep Now."

> It is afterwards
> and you talk on tiptoe
> happy to be part
> of the darkness,

lips becoming limp,
a prelude to tiredness.
Come close and sleep now,
for in the morning
when a policeman
disguised as the sun
creeps into the room:
and your mother
disguised as the birds
calls from the trees,
and you will put on a dress of guilt
and shoes with broken high ideals
and refusing coffee
run all the way home.[44]

That puts it very clearly and movingly. "Shoes with broken high ideals." We all wear them. What are we to do about it?

Well, the obvious thing is to forget about it. Just too bad it happened, but no point in making yourself miserable over spilt milk. Forget it. Ah, but that is not so easy. An estimated four people in ten are in a compulsive dependency on things like drugs, alcohol, pornography, gambling, and obsessive eating. Over three thousand million pills are issued annually by our doctors in order to counter depression and anxiety. People have pushed unwelcome aspects of their characters down into the subconscious, and those aspects have refused to go away; they continue to trouble us. We human beings are complicated creatures, and to repress our sense of guilt about the past solves nothing; it merely builds up trouble for the future.

And even if it didn't, we should still be in difficulty. Suppose you commit a murder and don't get caught; suppose you try to forget about it and are determined never to do such a thing again—what would happen if the evidence should come to light forty years later, as it has with some of the Nazi war

44. Roger McGough, lyrics from "Come Close and Sleep Now" in *Love, Love, Love* (Corgi, 1967). Used by permission.

criminals? The answer is simple: you would be guilty, however much you have tried to forget it, however long ago you did it, however hard you have tried to go straight in the meantime. Forgetting it does no good, even in the realm of human justice.

Then what is God to do about human failures? Is he to say, "Well, let's forget it"? Not the God I read about in the Bible! In a way, I wish he would; it would make it so much easier for me and, I suspect, for you. But on second thoughts, I am glad God is not like that—soft, spineless, devoid of justice, pretending that black is white and white is black when we all know perfectly well that is not the case. Yes, I'm glad God is holy and opposed to human wickedness. Heaven would be hell otherwise.

Not that it matters very much what I hope God may be like. I couldn't possibly know, unless he has revealed himself. And that he has done. He did it in personal terms, in Jesus Christ, no less, as we saw in chapter 9. And Jesus taught more severely about the judgment of God than any of the Old Testament prophets ever did. Remember, it was Jesus who taught about the two ways an individual could go: one led to God and the other to destruction. There were two groups a person could belong to: wheat, destined for the barn, or weeds, destined for the fire. There were two destinies that awaited everyone: inside the joyous feast or outside where there was weeping and gnashing of teeth. The teaching of Jesus flies straight in the face of our easygoing optimism that God is a good sort and won't be too fussy about achievements. He is good, and therefore he will be extremely fussy. He is the ethically upright God that our conscience uncomfortably suggests he is. He is deeply concerned at the fundamental difference between right and wrong and will not pretend that the distinction is unreal. He will by no means clear the guilty. The Almighty does not owe us forgiveness, any more than the world owes us a living. Forgiveness is never cheap.

Working our passage

All through the ages men and women have had an inkling of this fact. Forgiveness is never cheap; it is costly, and therefore they must do something to pay for it, to earn it. In a very real sense all religions have their root and their unity in this fact. We feel that we must *do* something, must achieve something, in order to atone for our failures, to make the Almighty gracious to us. All over the world, all through the ages, human beings have been trying to earn their passage to heaven. We say, in effect, "I live a good life. I do my best. Surely that is enough." The method we adopt to prove our point is immaterial. It may be through Eastern ways like the Eightfold Path, or mortification of the body in order to gain a better reincarnation. It may be through Western ways like trying harder, seeking to be decent, never doing anyone any harm, doing our best (and who can do more than that?).

This attempt to establish ourselves is exceptionally common in church circles. "I've been baptized and confirmed and married in church—and I send the kids to Sunday school. I go myself at Christmas—I mean, Christmas wouldn't be the same without going to church and singing those carols, would it?" In ways like this we pay our tiny premium for what we hope, when we stop to think about it, will be a really great heavenly insurance policy.

But despite its popularity, despite its prevalence all over the world, in every religious system and the irreligious ones as well, this road is a dead end. It is utterly misguided. And I will show you why.

It is shallow

This road of trying to earn our passage to heaven allows us to rely on deeds, not attitude. It is depressingly superficial and external. Would it satisfy any loving parents if their offspring kept the bedroom tidy and cleaned their shoes but never gave them a kiss, never spent time with them? Of course not. But are we to suppose that the heavenly Father will be overjoyed to welcome us when we haven't said so much as "Hello" to him from one year's end to the other, but smugly claim, "I've done lots of good things. I do my best. No one can do more"?

Listen to Jesus's analysis of the human condition. There is nothing external, superficial, or shallow about it. He says, "From within, out of men's hearts, come evil thoughts, sexual immorality, theft, murder ... arrogance and folly" (Mark 7:21–22 NIV). Of course we know how to do good things. But that does not change the fundamental twist in our natures: "You then, who are evil, know how to give good gifts to your children," observed the Master Physician (Luke 11:13). You cannot get rid of a cancerous growth by using lots of makeup and running around helping everyone else. It needs drastic surgery. Doing good deeds may well merely drive the dirt under the carpet. It is a very shallow remedy for the human situation.

"It is essential not to have faith in human nature," wrote Professor Butterfield, the famous historian. "Such a belief is very recent and very disastrous."[45] To reject the doctrine of human wickedness means that you will always be perplexed when you hear the perversity of men and women on the news each evening; you will always be puzzled by the prevalence of racism, by the exploitation of the helpless, by the oppression of the weak by the strong, and by the quirks in your own behavior. One celebrated atheist-turned-Christian put it like this: "To reject the doctrine of human sinfulness, as so many left-wing rationalists do, was to fall victim to the shallow optimism which led men to believe that the millennium was just round the corner, waiting to be introduced by a society of adequately psychoanalyzed, prosperous Socialists. It is because we rejected the doctrine of sin that we on the Left were always being disappointed."[46] So wrote Professor C. E. M. Joad after a

45. Herbert Butterfield, *Christianity and History* (Bell, 1950).
46. C. E. M. Joad, *God and Evil* (Faber and Faber, 1942).

lifetime of persuading himself that he was a good man at heart and that provided he did his best he'd be all right.

The truth is that our deeds cannot make up for ourselves. That is why Jesus hammered those good-living, religious Pharisees. It is all too possible to have a façade of goodness and religious observance but all the time to ignore the disease beneath. Jesus Christ demands a more radical solution.

It is impossible

You and I can't get to heaven by our own good deeds, for the simple reason that they are not good enough for God.

"What?" you say. "I'm a good-living person. I've kept the Ten Commandments." Have you? I wonder. Have you kept the first commandment of all, to give God the number one place in your life? I haven't. Jesus said it meant loving the Lord our God with all our heart and mind and soul and strength. I simply haven't begun to keep that first and greatest com- mandment. I break it every day. And that is not a very encouraging start as I set out to establish myself before God as a person who does his best and can't be expected to do more.

I glance down the other commandments. I must not make my own image of God? Well, I don't make graven images, of course. But I do tend to say, "I can't believe in a God who..." or, "The God I believe in is like this...." I make him in my image, rather than stopping to find out what he has revealed himself to be in the Bible.

I must not take the name of God in vain? I do it every day without thinking. Keep the Sabbath day holy, one day in seven separate for God and family and rest? Don't make me laugh. Honor father and mother? Not likely. When I'm young I rebel against them as hard as I can. When I'm married I neglect them. When they are old I stuff them in an old people's home. Honor them, indeed!

I feel a bit better seeing the command not to kill. I have never done that. But hang on a minute: didn't Jesus say something like the person who hates is just as repulsive to God as the one who gives vent to his hatred in murder? It's the same with that command about adultery. I may not actually have committed adultery, though it is extremely common in our society. But how about the lustful thoughts that run through my mind whenever I see a shapely woman? Yes, Jesus was right when he attributed those thoughts to the same weakness in human nature that produces adultery. "Thou shalt not steal." But I'm afraid I do. Steal goods from the shops, when nobody is looking; steal a free ride from the bus, when the conductor doesn't notice; steal from the tax system by getting paid in cash, not by check; yes, it happens. And as for not bearing false witness against my neighbor, why, that's what sells the Sunday papers. A little bit of scandal, a bit of exaggeration, of character assassination, of making myself look big in comparison with him. That final command against coveting, against unrestrained desire for what is not mine— why, the whole of our society is built on covetousness! You covet your neighbor's wife, his sports car, his vacation plans, his swimming pool.... Don't be stupid; life is built on coveting. Okay then, but don't run around and tell me that you have kept the Ten Commandments and are therefore a splendid person whom God ought to be proud to know. You have broken all of them. And so have I.

"Well, at any rate, I live by the Sermon on the Mount." It is amazing how many people think they do. I always feel they can't be serious. The standards of the Sermon on the Mount make the Ten Commandments look like kids' stuff. Do you hunger and thirst after what is right? Are you among the pure in heart who will see God? Are you a peacemaker at home and in industry? Do you allow yourself to be wronged, persecuted even, for the sake of what is right? Do you go and get reconciled with the colleague or neighbor whose guts you hate before presenting yourself in church with your offering? Are you perfect in undiscriminating concern for the good of all you meet, as your heavenly Father is, who makes his rain to fall equally on the just and unjust? "Don't be anxious about tomorrow: trust your Father, who looks after flowers and birds," says the sermon. Do you live like that? "Don't say, 'What shall we eat, or drink, or wear?' But seek first God's kingly rule and his righteousness, and all these things will be added to you," says the sermon. Do you live like that? No, of course you don't, and neither do I. Then we ought to be very careful when we boast that we live by the Sermon on the Mount. For that sermon concludes with the solemn assurance that if we do not follow the teaching Jesus presents here, we face ruin. Jesus says:

> Every one then who hears these words of mine and does them will be like a wise man who built his house upon the rock; and the rain fell, and the floods came, and the winds blew and beat upon that house, but it did not fall, because it had been founded on the rock. And every one who hears these words of mine and does not do them will be like a foolish man who built his house upon the sand; and the rain fell, and the floods came, and the winds blew and beat against that house, and it fell; and great was the fall of it.
> Matthew 7:24–27

On that day it will not do to say, "Lord, I did my best and even went to church from time to time." The sermon tells us he will reply,

> Not every one who says to me, "Lord, Lord," shall enter the kingdom of heaven, but he who does the will of my Father who is in heaven. On that day many will say to me, "Lord, Lord, did we not prophesy in your name, and cast out demons in your name, and do many mighty works in your name?" And then will I declare to them, "I never knew you; depart from me, you evildoers."
> Matthew 7:21–23

There sounds the death knell of everyone who attempts to justify themselves before God. It cannot be done. "Whoever keeps the whole law but fails in one point has become guilty of all of it," the Epistle of James says perceptively (2:10). After all, if I am caught for speeding, it won't help me to say that I have never robbed a bank and never mugged an old woman. I am guilty of speeding. I am in trouble. With God I have broken his law daily, hourly. I am in deep trouble. And it will be a very thin excuse to say, "I've done my best." For one thing, to be honest, I haven't. And for another, my best is not good enough for a holy God. I need something a lot better than my best if I'm going to get right with him. I find that the Bible is very unflattering about my attempts to doll myself up in the sight of God. It tells me that all my righteous acts (my righteous acts, mind you!) are like filthy rags, let alone the things I know are not much good. It implies that I have been looking in one of those distorting mirrors and hold too high a view of my own achievements and too low a view of God's nature and demands.

> The heart is deceitful above all things, and desperately corrupt; who can understand it? I the LORD search the mind and try the heart, to give to every man according to his ways, according to the fruit of his doings.
>
> Jeremiah 17:9–10

No, if that is the standard, if those are the stakes, then I can't compete. I begin to see that it is impossible that my best should be good enough for God.

It is intolerable

If heaven were the reward of merit, it would be ghastly. If I got there because I did my best, pushed my way in, and established my own claims no matter who got hurt in the process, it would be intolerable. If heaven were peopled by self-made men and women waving their own beastly goodness around under everyone's nose, it would be hell. The Academy Awards are bad enough, with everyone showing off their clothes for all they are worth. Is heaven to be one long awards ceremony? Perish the thought!

I found a gravestone once in an ancient church. It enshrined superbly this idea that I do my best and God ought to be very pleased with it, and it shows how repulsive that idea really is. It comes from King Ethelred the Unready, and it reads like this:

> I, Ethelred, king of Albion, in order that on the awful day of judgment I may, by the intercession of the saints, be deemed worthy to be admitted to the heavenly kingdom, do give Almighty God the possession of three lands [i.e., farms] to be held for ever for the monastery of the aforesaid martyr.

That shows up the proud attitude of "I do my best. What man can do more?" in its true colors. It is disgusting. God will not have his heaven cluttered up with the smug and the self-satisfied. The very idea is obscene.

Paul put it like this. Writing to some very self-satisfied Galatians, he said, in effect, "If you rely on trying your best in order to get to God, you have had it. You fall under the curse that the law of God imposes on all who break it. Does not the Old Testament say, 'Cursed be every one who does not abide by *all* things written in the book of the law, and do them'? You cannot claim obedience like that, can you? Very well, you fall under the judgment of God." In other words, it is impossible to get through to God on the basis of my own good works. But Paul does not leave it there. He goes on in the very next verse to show that even if it were possible, it would be intolerable. It would mean that anyone could put a pistol at God's head, so to speak, and say, "I've done all these good things. You must make room for me in your heaven, even though I have never given you a thought and don't love you the least bit." So Paul maintains, "It is quite obvious that nobody gets in touch with God just by doing good things. That would leave the whole principle of trust out of the equation. And the Old Testament

"I do my best. No one can do more

130

makes it quite clear that if you want to live w
must be on the basis of loving trust. But dc
nothing to do with this attitude of trust; it is
cold achievement." That is a rough parapl
3:10–12. And it seems to me to be unanswe
doing my best to put me in the clear with God, I shall find not
only that it is impossible, because I fail again and again and
again, but that the whole idea is intolerable because it leaves
me untouched in my pride and self-esteem and takes no
account of the loving trust I should have in my heavenly
Father.

Unpalatable truth

In a word, all attempts to establish myself before God are
bound to fail. He is holy and I am not. My good deeds cannot
make up for my crooked heart and my rebellious attitude
toward the God I have wronged and from whose gaze I am
only too anxious to escape. It is hard and humiliating to have
to admit this. That is why so many people prefer to shelter
under the bogus refuge of "I do my best. No one can do more."
But unless I have a better shelter than that, it will let the wind
and the rain and the hail in at the day of judgment. I need to
come to the position of one rich, able, intelligent, young
pleasure seeker, sixteen centuries ago, who was big enough to
face up to the unpalatable truth and get right with God on
God's terms, not his own. He wrote, "You took me, God, from
behind my own back where I had put myself all the time I
preferred not to see myself. And you set me before my face, that
I might see how vile I was. I saw myself, and was horrified."[47]
That was Augustine, who later became the famous Christian
leader. I fancy we all need to tread that humbling path, if God is
to be able to do anything with us. He has no room for swelled

47. St. Augustine, *The Confessions of St. Augustine*, trans. Rex Warner (Signet
Classics, 2001).

...ads in his family. There is one condition for entry, one only. It is to change our attitude, to come down off our high horse, and be willing to trust him and his way of pardon. What that is we shall see in the next chapter.

11

"Nothing can change the past."

This chapter is a companion piece to the previous one. Both of them deal with the reactions of human beings to guilt. In the last chapter we were looking at the person who hoped the past would go away, as long as he did his best. In this chapter we are concerned with the person who knows all too well that the past will not go away. It is permanent. Nothing can change it. Its stain is indelible. Often one hears a person bewail some awful incident in their past and say, "I can never forgive myself." Like Lady Macbeth after the murder, they continue, as it were, forever going through the motions of washing their hands, but they are all too well aware that all the perfumes of Arabia cannot remove the accusing smell of blood. Nothing can undo the past.

Their problem, then, is precisely the opposite of the one we looked at in the previous chapter. There the "self-made man" was confident that he would be all right; he did his best, and what more could be required of him? Here, nothing avails to put the past right. But paradoxical as it may seem, both diseases have the same remedy. It is to be found on a green hill far away, outside a city wall.

The cross

Using your imagination, come with me to that famous scene. It is a bank holiday. A rough, laughing crowd jostles through the narrow streets of Jerusalem. At last the Roman governor has ratified the decision of the Jewish Council and sentenced Jesus of Nazareth. He is to die in the approved fashion for criminals of the lower classes in occupied countries: by crucifixion. If you have seen Mel Gibson's brutal film, *The Passion of the Christ*, you will know what an appallingly barbaric form of execution this was. The victim is first flogged to within an inch of his life and then led out to die. Imagine it. The knot of soldiers in charge of the execution pushes through the crowd. Of the three prisoners they are guarding carefully, one stumbles. He has been kept awake all night without food or drink and has had a succession of trials. He is exhausted. He collapses under the weight of the heavy crossbeam of his cross, which he has to carry. The lack of sleep and food and the loss of blood from his back, lacerated by the Roman cat-o'-nine-tails, prove too much for him. He stumbles to his knees, and the soldiers grab a black man who happens to be passing by. "You'll do; carry his cross, and look sharp about it."

Soon the execution party comes to a spot outside the city wall, while the crowd watches the spectacle of three public deaths with mingled emotions. The soldiers dig pits for the crosses to go into. The crosses are laid on the ground, and the three men are made to lie on them. Long iron spikes are then nailed through their ankles and their wrists. Some years ago the bones of a man crucified only a few years after Jesus were unearthed in Israel. None had been discovered before. The spikes had pierced through the two bones at the wrist and had gone through the ankle. I was aghast when I saw them. Think of the agony it must have been. No doubt the two criminals executed with Jesus cursed and swore and struggled. Jesus breathed a prayer instead: "Father, forgive them. They do not know what they are doing."

The grisly job is done at length. The soldiers lift the crosses one by one and slot them into the ground. The men are now exposed to the gaze of the crowd, suspended between earth and sky, with every nerve in agony, fighting for breath. No quick death awaits them, as they hang in terrible anguish, parched by the heat, distraught by the flies.

A God-forsaken place

What accounts for the fascination that central figure on the cross has exercised over nineteen centuries of history? It could not be merely his physical suffering, ghastly as that was. Other men have died in pain as great as his, perhaps greater. The two brigands executed with him had just as terrible an end. No, his physical sufferings do not get us to the heart of what was achieved on that cross. Interestingly enough, the Gospel writers hardly pause on them at all. "There they crucified him," is all they say, sparing us the harrowing detail. Nor can his mental suffering exhaust the mystery. How galling to have priests mocking him:

> He saved others; he cannot save himself. He is the King of Israel; let him come down now from the cross, and we will believe in him. He trusts in God; let God deliver him now, if he desires him; for he said, "I am the Son of God."
>
> Matthew 27:42–43

How heartbreaking to find all his disciples running for cover. How humiliating to be exposed as a failure, his life's work in ruins. How crushing to be rejected and crucified by God's own people whom he had come to teach and to rescue. His mental sufferings must have broken his heart, but they do not penetrate the mystery of that cross.

Darkness falls, a premature darkness, a darkness that could be felt. Curiously enough, a pagan historian, Thallus, records it, so it is no mere colorful exaggeration from the Gospels. But, nonetheless, it is highly symbolic of the darkness that engulfed Jesus at that supreme moment of his life. Darkness pierced with his cry of agony, culled from Psalm 22:1 (NIV): "My God, my God, why have you forsaken me?" Darkness matched only by that in the Garden of Gethsemane the night before, when he

had faced up to his death and what it would entail, and had
sweated blood at the prospect. Why indeed was this best of
men allowed to feel bereft, God-forsaken in this his finest hour?
The answer, which all different strands of the New Testament
give, is this: he *felt* cut off from his heavenly Father for the
simple reason that he *was* cut off. Paul, as we saw in the last
chapter, was clear that no man could approach God dressed in
the clothes of his own good deeds. Because all have broken the
law of God, all rest under its curse, its judgment. But if you were
to ask Paul what lay at the heart of the cross of Jesus, he would
tell you: "Christ redeemed us from the curse of the law, *having
become a curse for us*" (Gal. 3:13, emphasis added). Unthinkable—that the Holy One, the perfect man, the innocent Son of
God should end up in the place of judgment, of cursing. But so
it was.

As a Jew, Paul would have known his Old Testament. He
knew very well that passage in Deuteronomy, which said that
anyone exposed on a "tree" must be seen as resting under the
curse of God. He had felt, in his pre-Christian days, that here
was an excellent reason why Jesus could not possibly be the
longed-for Messiah of his people; he had ended up not merely
in the place of failure but in the place of cursing. On the road to
Damascus Paul had met the risen Lord Jesus. He had had his
previous view shattered. He came to see that Jesus had indeed
come to meet his death in the place of cursing, but *the curse was
ours!* And he gladly bore it for us. No wonder Paul gives up his
life in glad service for "the Son of God who loved me and gave
himself for me." As he reflects on the fantastic exchange of
positions that Jesus undertook for us, he can do nothing else.

> For our sake he [God] made him to be sin who knew no sin, so
> that in him we might become the righteousness of God.
>
> 2 Corinthians 5:21

No wonder Jesus felt cut off from God; he *was* cut off . . . and it
was in order to enable us to come near.

What does it mean?

The New Testament writers struggle to express this undreamed-of good news in a variety of metaphors. Fantastic that God should underwrite our debts and lift our burdens and endure our curse and carry our guilt. Fantastic, indeed, but it takes us to the very heart of Calvary. That is why Jesus steadfastly set his face to go to Jerusalem—when he might so easily have left for somewhere else. He had an appointment with death. He knew that he was going to endure the destiny of the Suffering Servant, sketched out so graphically in the Old Testament prophecies. He knew that the Lord was going to lay on him the iniquities of us all. He knew that he was going to bear our offenses. He knew that the lashes, which meant our peace, would lacerate him. He knew that his death would be a sacrifice for sin, such as no sacrificial system in the world could match— the Lord, offering his life for sinners. He knew that the Son of Man, as he called himself, would give his life as ransom for many on that cross. He knew that he would see the fruit of his labors, after it was all over, and be satisfied—feel it was worth it. For he was about to forge a new agreement between God and humanity, a new covenant. All other covenants in the history of religions had two sides to them, our side and God's side. That was just the trouble with them—men and women kept breaking their side of the bargain! But this covenant would bring forgiveness of sins. It would undertake not only God's side but our side as well. On that cross he would be the perfect man, offering up his life for others; he would also be the perfect God, for "God was reconciling the world to himself in Christ, not counting men's sins against them" (2 Cor. 5:19 NIV). Such was the divine plan, hidden from all eternity in the purposes of God but revealed in its horror and its glory on the first Good Friday.

Perhaps we could do worse than look at it from the perspective of three people present that day. It will give us three

pictures, three metaphors of what Jesus achieved for us on that
cross; three ways of enabling us to see that even if we can't
forgive ourselves for some terrible thing we have done in the
past, God can and will forgive, and do so with perfect justice
and with boundless love.

The freedom fighter's view

There was one person on that first Good Friday who vividly
came to understand what the cross of Jesus meant. He was a
freedom fighter, caught in the act of armed insurrection and
murder. Imprisoned with his companions, he awaited the day
of execution, glad that he had knocked off a few Romans, sad
that he had not managed to deliver his country from the
clutches of Rome. Imagine him there in his cell, sweating with
fear as that last morning of his life dawned. The steps along the
corridor. The key in the lock. And the hairs on his neck stood
up. Then to his amazement, the centurion knocked the chains
off his hands and feet and said, "You're a free man, Barabbas.
Get out of here." Incredulously, Barabbas looked at him and
concluded it was a sick joke. But it was no joke. He'd heard
of Pilate's strange offer to release to the people at that Feast of
Passover either himself or another revolutionary leader of a
very different kind, another "Barabbas," which means "son of
the father." Dazed, he would have hardly been able to drag
himself away from the place of execution where his friends
were dying for the crimes they had committed on behalf of
their country, and where this strange Son of the Father was
dying on Barabbas's very own cross, in Barabbas's very own
place. History does not relate what became of him. But he
could scarcely have missed the point that Jesus was taking his
place. Jesus's death was settling his account so that his crimes
would never be brought up against him again. He could
scarcely have avoided reflecting that by rights he should have
been on that central cross. "He did it for me," I can imagine
him saying. "He did it for me."

That strange exchange made its impression on the Christian community. The apostle Peter was almost certainly an eyewitness to the scene, skulking at the edge of the crowd where he would not attract unwanted attention. He tells us in his first letter that he was a "witness of the sufferings of Christ" (1 Pet. 5:1). After seeing Jesus carrying that cross up to the place of execution, stumbling under its weight, nailed to its unwelcome embrace, he wrote to his Christian readers words that are surely to be interpreted in the light of what he saw and felt that day.

He committed no sin; no guile was found on his lips. When he was reviled, he did not revile in return; when he suffered, he did not threaten; but he trusted to him who judges justly. He himself bore our sins in his body on the tree. . . . By his wounds you have been healed.

1 Peter 2:22–24

Images of the Suffering Servant of Isaiah, of Jesus staggering up to Golgotha bearing the load of Peter's sins, of the innocent Jesus in the place of us guilty Barabbases, may all have struggled through his mind as he wrote. He put it with great clarity in the next chapter:

For Christ also died for sins once for all, the righteous for the unrighteous, that he might bring us to God.

1 Peter 3:18

That was why he died: the righteous in the place of the unrighteous. Peter had understood what the cross was all about.

So had Paul. In a remarkable passage in his letter to the Colossians, he tells us that God has forgiven us all our sins, having canceled the list of failures that stood against our names, with its legal demands; he swept it aside, nailing it to his cross. What a sublime understanding of Calvary! There was a long list of crimes against Barabbas, but Jesus met them all when he died in Barabbas's place on that central cross. There was a long list of much more refined sins against Paul's name, but Jesus met them all when he died in Paul's place, on that central cross. The condemned criminal usually had a charge sheet with his crime written on it hung around his neck as he went out to execution; this was nailed onto his cross. And Paul sees Jesus going out to die—not with the jeering accusation "King of the Jews" around his neck but with Paul's sins, your sins, and my sins hung around his neck. That is why he died. To square our account. To clear our debt to the God we have wronged. He swept aside all the accusing failures that I have written against myself through my willful sins, and he nailed them to Christ's cross. They will never be raised again with me, any more than they will with Paul or other Christian believers. For Christ has once died for sins, the righteous for the unrighteous, so as to bring us to God. That is one aspect of the meaning of the cross. It settles our debts. It sweeps them aside. It means they will never be raised against us again. For God in Christ has paid the account to the last penny, even though it took him to that bitter cross in order to do so. Nothing we can do can change our guilty past. But this act of supreme generosity on his part has changed everything.

The executioner's view

There was another most interesting character at that cross. We do not know his name, but he made his own impression on the Christian community, for the story is told in no less than three of the Gospels. He was the centurion in charge of the execution squad. He had the closest view of anyone on that grim occasion. He watched Jesus suffer with dignity. He noticed that Jesus was concerned entirely for others: the soldiers who had nailed him there, the mother who had borne him, and the criminals executed with him. He had heard the priests mocking Jesus; he had seen the crowd jeering. He had felt the uncanny darkness; he had heard the great cry as Jesus died. And he burst out with a confession of faith in this man he had just executed. "Truly this was the Son of God" is the phrase Matthew (27:54) and Mark (15:39) record. Luke's account is more politically slanted: "Certainly this man was innocent" (23:47). Maybe he said both, convinced not only of the innocence of Jesus but of his superhuman quality. Exactly what a Roman centurion would have meant by "Son of God" we cannot be sure. It was one of the titles by which the emperor liked to be known, so any utterance of it was a fantastic confession of loyalty to a crucified member of a subject race. But we can hardly doubt that the New Testament writers meant us to see far more in that cry. It was the primitive Christian confession: Jesus Christ is the Son of God and Savior. Here, the man who had killed Jesus was recognizing in him the way back to God!

I think we can be pretty sure that this interpretation is correct. In the verses immediately preceding, the New Testament writers do a curious but deliberate thing. First, they record the death of Jesus: "Jesus breathed his last" (Mark 15:37 NIV). They then seem to ruin this climax of their story by a ludicrous bit of irrelevant information: at that moment "the curtain of the temple was torn in two from top to bottom" (Mark 15:38 NIV). They then come back to Calvary and tell us of the centurion's confession of faith. What are they trying to convey?

It is not difficult to discover, once we recall what the curtain in the temple was for. It was intended to guard the holiest part of the temple from intruders. Nobody was to go into that Holy of Holies except the high priest, once a year, on the Day of Atonement. He then made sacrifice for his own sins and for the sins of the people by shedding the blood of an animal and offering it on the altar. The curtain meant exclusion; it meant that God was holy, and man was not. It was a vast visual aid to get one simple message across, that God is too holy for sinful folk like you and me to approach. It spelled, "Keep out."

When Jesus died on that cross, the temple curtain was split; it was an act of God and was probably due to an earthquake that the Jewish historian Josephus says took place about that time and shook the lintels of the temple. But however it happened, its message was loud and clear to those New Testament writers.

It spelled, "Come in." It meant that Jesus, the supreme High Priest, had made the ultimate sacrifice not for his own sins (he had none to atone for) but for those of a whole world gone astray. It meant that those who trusted him could now draw near to God without fear that they would be excluded. And listen to the way that confident access resounds through the New Testament. "Now in Christ Jesus you who once were far off have been brought near in the blood of Christ," says the letter to the Ephesians (2:13), and "through him we both [Jews and Gentiles alike] have access in one Spirit to the Father" (2:18). In his letter to the Romans, Paul thrills to the wonder of our acquittal through what Jesus did on that cross. "We have peace with God through our Lord Jesus Christ," he cried. "Through him we have obtained access" (Rom. 5:1–2). And the writer to the Hebrews puts it a bit more allegorically but very powerfully, when he writes:

> We have confidence to enter the sanctuary by the blood of Jesus, by the new and living way which opened for us through the curtain, that is, through his flesh.
>
> Hebrews 10:19–20

His flesh offered for us on that cross made the way into God's holy presence possible; it split the curtain, so to speak, which kept God so distant and unreal. And instead of one man going in once a year after due sacrifice—repeated annually—we can all go in at any time. There is unrestricted access into the holy presence of God for all who trust the one whose death made it all possible. That death meant access. And we find the centurion making no delay to take advantage of that access—achieved through the death of Jesus for which he had been responsible. We are meant to see ourselves in that centurion, just as we are meant to see ourselves in Barabbas. The death of Jesus settles our account and means we can go straight into the presence of God, unafraid, knowing that the barriers have been broken down, the guilt has been expiated, the dirt washed away by the death of Jesus, the Savior. And that is good news for troubled consciences, which no psychiatry can match.

The dying robber's view

The third figure at the cross of Jesus who catches our attention is the robber who hangs beside him. As they suffer there together, this man makes the most remarkable statement in the whole astounding narrative. He says, "Jesus, remember me when you come into your kingdom" (Luke 23:42 NIV). The other criminal executed alongside them had been cursing at the silent sufferer. "Messiah, are you? Okay then, save yourself—and us!" But the man we have come to know as the penitent thief rebuked him. "Do you not fear God? You are going to meet him soon enough! And neither you nor I can complain; we are getting what we deserve. But this man has done nothing wrong." It was then that he turned to Jesus with his fascinating request: "Jesus, remember me when you come into your kingdom" (see Luke 23:39–43). What a fantastic example of faith that was. To believe that the man executed alongside you had a future and would be able to remember you. To believe that he had a kingdom and would come into his kingly rule. To turn to a bloodied, suffering man in his death throes and ask for favorable memory in the life to come—I find it staggering. But that is what he did. And Jesus replied with one of the greatest of all his sayings: "Today you will be with me in paradise" (Luke 23:43 NIV). It was marvelous for the thief to know that he would die today; often men lingered on for a day or two after crucifixion. Marvelous to have that future described in a lovely old Persian word for a park or garden, the garden of God. But most marvelous of all is the implication that, though unspoken, comes through like a trumpet blast. This man's accusing past will be silenced; his guilt will be expiated; his sins will be forgotten. He will be with Jesus in God's garden. He had done nothing to deserve it. How could he do anything to earn his forgiveness when he was hanging there on a cross, dying? What could he contribute to his own salvation—except the sin from which he needed to be saved? But that, the apostle Luke would seem to teach us, is precisely the condition of being forgiven. "Nothing in my hand I bring: simply to Thy cross I cling."[48] It is not the clergymen with lots of religious accreditations to their name; it is not the Romans with all their political power and influence; but it is a simple, guilty, condemned criminal who finds pardon through Jesus.

Do ... or done?

That is why the New Testament writers make such a point of telling us that we are not put right with God by anything that we do: rather by something done for us. The worldly individual's religion has two letters in it: "do." The forgiven sinner's has four: "done." And in that "done," countless people of every age and culture have found peace. "There is no condemnation for those who are in Christ Jesus," writes Paul. "For what our attempts to keep the law could never do, God himself has done through the person and the death of Jesus." That is a rough paraphrase of Romans 8:1–2. Done!

Let me be very direct and ask you an embarrassing question. If you died tonight, why should God accept you into his heaven? How, I wonder, would you reply? If you are just a churchgoer, if you are an I-do-my-best type, you would surely hesitate before answering. You would be suitably modest and noncommittal. But the believer can say with joy and confidence, "I know I would be accepted if I died tonight. Indeed, I am accepted now, and I have many promises of the New Testament to assure me of it. You see, I am trusting not in anything I *do* for acceptance with God but on what he has *done*. That is why I can be sure about it. My future is guaranteed by Calvary."

48. *Rock of Ages, Cleft for Me*, words: Augustus M. Toplady, 1776; music: Thomas Hastings, 1830.

Questions

It is at this point that questions flood in. Is the cross all that necessary, you ask? Listen. Some years ago I had meningitis; it is a killer disease. Of course, I did not know I was so ill. I just had a splitting headache. But when the top physician in Durban came to see me in the middle of a Sunday afternoon in the middle of his holiday and rushed me to the hospital, you did not need to persuade me I was ill! If that man had to be called in, I must have been in a serious condition. And if nothing less would suffice than the coming to earth and the death on the cross of Jesus, the Great Physician, then we must have been in a bad way. Don't you think that if there had been any other possible way of rescuing us, God would have taken it?

Perhaps you feel that the cross of Christ is unfair. Does it almost seem that God is punishing Jesus instead of us? It is not like that. Actually, the New Testament never speaks of God punishing Jesus on the cross. It does speak of his bearing our sins there. It does speak of his doing so in our place and for our sake. But we must not think of three parties, as it were: God sitting comfortably up in heaven; Jesus in agony on the cross; and you and I going free as a result. No. The Bible says that God was very much involved in what happened on that cross. "God was in Christ, reconciling the world to himself." He was coming in person to deal with the mess we had gotten ourselves into. It also tells us that *we* were very much involved with what happened there. Jesus was our representative; he was truly one of us, bearing the consequences of humanity's rebellion. And just as he died and rose again, so those who come to him have a standing call to share in his death (i.e., allow him to nail our old, sinful nature to the cross, so to speak) and in his resurrection (i.e., allow the power of his risen life to set us free from the well-worn grooves of bad habits). Yes, God the Father and we ourselves are very much involved in the cross of Jesus Christ. It would be most misleading and crude to suggest that God "took it out on" Jesus for us. Rather, God was in Christ on the cross, allowing our rebellion to crush him. Such was his love.

Very well then, what happens to those who have never had a chance to hear the gospel? The New Testament makes it plain that Jesus died not for our sins only but for the sins of the whole world. That death was for believers who died in ignorance of the cross in the centuries that went before. It was for the great heroes and heroines of faith in the Old Testament days, people like Abraham and Sarah and David. They could sing, "Blessed is he whose transgressions are forgiven, whose sins are covered" (Ps. 32:1 NIV) because they trusted that God would find a way to do just that. They did not understand how he could, but they trusted in him and not in their own fancied goodness. No doubt it will be the same for people after the coming of Jesus, those who have never heard the gospel, if they genuinely trust in God and not in their own good deeds to save them. The cross was for them too. And when they hear of it, as they sometimes do through a Bible or a missionary, they rejoice and thank the great God who had found such a marvelous way to settle their debts, grant them pardon, and secure their access to him. But that does not let us off the hook, does it? We have heard the message of his love and what he did for us on the cross. The only proper question is, What are we going to do about it?

"But, surely, I don't need to do anything about it?" you may be asking. "Doesn't the whole thrust of your argument mean that I am automatically forgiven through what has been done for me on the cross?" Not so. Forgiveness is costly. It always involves two parties. As the singer Elton John says in one of his most profound songs: "Sorry seems to be the hardest word."[49] A pardon may be offered, but it has to be accepted. As we saw earlier, a governor's pardon offered to some prisoner is quite

49. *Sorry Seems to Be the Hardest Word,* words: Bernie Taupin, music: Elton John, © 1976 Big Pig Music Limited.

void until it is accepted. I would be a fool if I ignored it. I would be stupid to take it for granted and assume that naturally I would be entitled to a pardon. I would be mad to say, "What a beautiful document: I will frame it and use it to decorate the wall of my cell." I would be out of my mind to tear it up. Obviously, I need to accept it with gratitude and humility. That is just what you need to do with the pardon that God holds out to you in the cross of Jesus Christ. It will do you no good if you take it for granted, or if you say in admiration, "How wonderful." It will do you no good if you ignore it all your life. It will do you no good if you tear it up and throw it in the face of the donor. One dying thief was forgiven so that nobody need despair, however bad his past has been, however short his grasp on life. But only one was forgiven, as if to remind us that nobody can dare to assume the pardon of God without accepting it personally. The cross of Jesus stands between those two thieves. One was saved and the other lost. The cross of Jesus is equally divisive in today's world. Some know they are guilty but know equally that because of what he did on that cross they are forgiven. Others try to pretend that they are all right, and that they do not need a pardon, do not need to ask Jesus to change the past. The cross divides those two groups of people. Which group do you belong to? Don't rest until you get the matter clear. Mercifully it is possible to move from one group to the other. If a dying thief can discover a pardon at the cross, so can you. Don't miss it, for this is the only medicine in the world that can change your guilty past.

12

"When you're dead, you're dead!"

"When I die, I rot," said Bertrand Russell.[50] And you can't argue with that. It is obviously true. But is it the whole truth? Does the real "me" disappear?

An intriguing question

Every few years one of the major daily or Sunday papers takes the matter up. They run a series on THE GREAT MYSTERY OF LIFE AFTER DEATH or some such title. The insurance companies take it up, with all their loaded advertising about "Refuge for Life." The question of life after the grave has intrigued men and women since the earliest dawn of the human race. I remember seeing some of the oldest tombs in existence at Byblos in Lebanon. The skeletons were buried in a position highly indicative of their hope of an afterlife. Their knees were tucked up under their chins, and they were encased in an earthenware egg. In other words, the people of that far-off day cherished the hope that new life would break out of that egg of death. They hoped that after you were dead you might somehow live again.

I remember being fascinated on a visit to Italy by the preoccupation with this subject among the Romans. Among the many mosaics, there is one particularly memorable picture of the phoenix, a mythical bird that was supposed to come to life

50. Bertrand Russell, *The Autobiography* (Routledge, 2000).

again after it had been burned on the funeral pyre. Underneath the picture, the artist had written, "Phoenix, how lucky you are!"

To be sure, when you're dead, you're dead. It is very final. There is no return to life. But is it the end of you? Or is there a life beyond? It is a fascinating question.

But there's another side to it.

A threatening question

If there is a life after death, what will it be like? It is bad enough if death is the end, but far worse if it is not. Epicurus, the Greek pleasure-loving philosopher, said long ago, "What men fear is not that death is annihilation, but that it is not." And William Butler Yeats, in his poem "Death," catches the feeling precisely:

> Nor dread nor hope attend
> A dying animal.
> A man awaits his end,
> Dreading and hoping all.[51]

What if we shall be called to account for the lives we have lived? What if, as Hebrews 9:27 puts it, "it is appointed for men to die once, and after that comes judgment"? Perish the thought—it would be too awful! But it would be fair, would it not? It would match our freedom. We know all too well that freedom and accountability are the two sides of the same coin. A student has almost unlimited freedom; but the day comes when he or she has to give an account of it during final exams. An architect has enormous freedom in designing and building a house. But at the end of the day he is accountable to his employer. What if life is like that? What if it should be true that every one of us shall give an account of himself to God?

51. William Butler Yeats, *The Collected Poems of W. B. Yeats* (Wordsworth Editions, 2000).

What if Jesus is right in his story of the rich fool (Luke 12:16–20)? He lived as though this life was all there is; he made success and money and property his gods and left God out. And then one night he died. God said to him,

> You fool! This very night your life will be demanded from you. Then who will get what you have prepared for yourself?
>
> Luke 12:20 NIV

A devastating story, very apt for our materialistic age. Could Jesus be right? If so, it would not be much fun to have God saying, "You fool" to you. I saw an advertisement for life insurance some time ago, advising me to invest in the company, and it ended with this sardonic note: "Let those who think they are going to live forever make their own arrangements." What if we do live on—and have not made any arrangements for such a contingency?

What if Jesus is right in his story of the rich man and Lazarus (Luke 16:19–31)? What if there is a life after the grave and we are accountable for the way we have lived in this one—for our selfishness, our callous disregard of the needs of the Lazaruses on our doorstep (not to mention the half of the world's population who live in poverty because of the economic policies pursued by the greedy West)? What if we shall be judged on that day by the way we have treated the Asian bus driver, the homeless, or the old person suffering from senility in the local nursing home? Of course, prejudice, including racism, is a two-way road. One black Christian leader challenged his fellow blacks like this: "At the judgment day, the Lord will say to us, 'Why didn't you preach the gospel to all those poor whites, lost in affluence and ambition?' " What if such an unpalatable possibility turned out to be true, after all?

"Ah," you say, "it is all sheer speculation. How can you possibly know?"

A question that can be answered

One could only know if there is a life beyond the grave if
someone came back with reliable information. And that is, by
definition, impossible. Dead men don't rise. When you're dead,
you're dead. But this brings us to the very heart of the Christian
claim. Alone among the religions of the world, Christianity
dares to maintain that we can know about life after death, we
can know how to get there, we can know something of what
awaits us, for the simple and sufficient reason that Jesus Christ,
crucified on the cross, rose again from the grave.

Now this is a preposterous claim. It cannot be true. Or can it?
There is, of course, only one way of finding out whether or not
there is a life beyond the grave. And that would be for someone
to die and come back to tell us what it is like. I suppose it is a bit
like space exploration. The moon has fascinated human beings
from time immemorial. Was there, or was there not, life on this
mysterious world of the moon? What were conditions like on
the side of the moon we cannot see? Nobody could tell, though
that did not stop lots of guessing. Nobody could tell until Neil
Armstrong, the first person to land on the moon, came back to
tell us what it is like. Not only that, but he paved the way for
later space travelers to follow.

The Christian claim

Now that is precisely how the Christian claim about life after
death can be assessed. We believe that one man, Jesus of
Nazareth, came back from beyond the grave to show us that
he has overcome the last enemy and to enable us to follow in
his footsteps. Of course, we know that dead people are not
in the habit of rising from their tombs. We know that there is
no scientifically established category of dead men who have
come back to life again. We are not naive; we know that our
claim boggles the imagination. But we believe it all the same,
and on good evidence. I will give you some of that evidence in

a moment. But for now let's be clear about one thing. We are not making this claim for any old Tom, Dick, or Harry. We are maintaining that in one person, one very special person, one who was more than human, the forces of death met their match. We saw in chapter 9 strong reasons for supposing that Jesus was not only human but also divine. How can we be dogmatic in asserting that he could not rise from the grave, in that case? We saw that he lived an absolutely unspoiled and perfect life. How can we be so sure that a life that gave no foothold to sin could not master death? We have no others to compare it with. Jesus made his whole credibility rest upon the assertion that he would "do a Jonah" on his contemporaries, and just as Jonah came back from his three-day "death" inside the great fish, so he himself would rise from the jaws of death (Matt. 12:39–41). So let us lay aside blind prejudice that says, "It couldn't happen," and see whether, according to all the evidence, it *did* happen in this one solitary case of Jesus. If he was perfectly human, if he was more than human, we cannot rule it out.

I have tried to look at the evidence in some detail in a book called *The Empty Cross of Jesus*. You might care to follow the matter up there. But here are five points to consider, as you reflect on the events on that first Good Friday.

1. The prisoner was dead
Very dead. Roman executions were grimly thorough. As a matter of fact, the officer in charge of the execution was himself liable to the death penalty if his job was not done efficiently. In the case of Jesus, the execution squad saw that he was dead already and so did not bother to break his legs (a barbaric way of ensuring the crucified wretches did not continue to raise themselves on the crosses and gulp in air). But just to make doubly sure, they pierced his side with a spear, and out came "blood and water" as an eyewitness put it (John 19:34–37). This is a fascinating detail, all the more

remarkable because the writer could have no idea of its medical significance. But any doctor now will tell you that the separation of the blood into clot and serum is one of the surest indications of death. That is what John records, even though he could only marvel at it, not understand it. But it gives proof positive that Jesus was dead. If we wanted more, we could have it; not only did the centurion report to the governor that the job was done (and he knew a dead man when he saw one—he had dispatched enough of them), but Pilate himself allowed Joseph of Arimathea to take the body away (John 19:38). It is another fascinating touch to discover that the word here used for the "body" of Jesus is, in the original Greek, "corpse"; the word is never used of a live person, always of a dead one.

Yes, Jesus was dead, all right. So any variety of the "swoon theory," which suggests Jesus recovered from his terrible ordeal in the cool of the tomb and crept out, is utterly discredited. It simply couldn't have happened. But so keen have unbelievers been to reject the plain teaching of the New Testament writers (even though it is based on eyewitness testimony), they have resorted to theories that maintain that Jesus was not really dead. You find it as long ago as Celsus in the second century. He was a strong anti-Christian who explained the resurrection by supposing that Jesus was nursed back to health by Mary Magdalene; forty days later his wounds got the better of him, and he died and was buried secretly, but not before he had assembled his friends and walked off into a cloud on a mountaintop! Such poverty-stricken explanations are still put forward from time to time. They are invalidated based on the massive evidence that Jesus was indeed dead. They are also psychologically improbable, in the extreme. Would disciples who knew that Jesus had never risen from the tomb, but had died ignominiously from his wounds, have gone all over the world proclaiming his risen presence with such joy that people felt they might be drunk, and with such persistence that prison, torture, and death could not stop them? You don't let yourself be bumped off for a fraud.

2. The tomb was empty

Very empty, on that first Easter morning. And nobody has ever been able to suggest a really plausible explanation, apart from the united testimony of every strand in the New Testament that the tomb was empty because Jesus had conquered death and was alive again.

Of course, people have tried to explain it away. One distinguished professor suggested that, in the mist of early dawn, Mary and her friends found the wrong tomb! Did she not do better later, we might ask? Was Joseph of Arimathea equally clueless on the location of his own personal tomb, which he had given over to Jesus? Another crude suggestion, made as early as the end of the second century, has at least a touch of humor about it. It suggests that the gardener was responsible for all the talk about the resurrection of Jesus. He was so fed up at sightseers stomping around the tomb, treading all over the seedlings he had planted, that he removed the body and buried it elsewhere! Another rationalization of the empty tomb appears in the New Testament itself. The soldiers, set to guard the tomb, were bribed by embarrassed Jewish authorities to spread a false report about how the body of Jesus had disappeared. So, the soldiers circulated the story that after they had fallen asleep on duty, the disciples came and stole Jesus's body (Matt. 28:11–15)!

But all of these attempts to explain away the empty tomb on the assumption that someone stole the body come apart very fast, on this simple point. There were only two groups of people interested in what became of the body of this executed teacher: his friends and his enemies. The records all show us that Jesus's friends had no idea that he might rise; they were not expecting anything of the sort. Rather, they scattered sadly like any other band whose hopes had been dashed by the death of their leader. There was no expectation in Judaism that any prophet or teacher might personally come back from the grave, though there was the hope of a general resurrection on the last day. His disciples were not expecting his resurrection. What's more, if they had been able to spirit the body away (despite the strict guard kept on the tomb), they would scarcely have been prepared to die for their fraud; nor would people all over the world and in all generations from then till now be so confident that Jesus lives.

But if it was not the disciples who stole the body, how could it have been the opposition? They had been scheming for Jesus's execution for ages. And now it had happened. The last thing they would have done is give occasion to any talk about resurrection by moving his body surreptitiously. They had him where they wanted him, dead and buried. We may be sure they spared no effort to keep him there—hence the seal and the guard on the tomb. To suggest that either the Jews or the Romans moved his body is a shallow man's safeguard from having to admit the truth of the resurrection. Had they been so incredibly foolish, they would only have had to produce the body of Jesus, when the disciples claimed his resurrection, in order to squash the new movement at a single stroke. And this is what nobody was able to do. They just got very cross with the apostles, tried to silence them, put them in prison, and tortured and killed them. But they could not discredit their story that the tomb was empty for the good reason that Jesus had risen.

Did you ever notice the fascinating bit of corroborative detail in the apostle John's account of the resurrection? He tells with artless simplicity of Peter and the beloved disciple racing to the sepulcher to see for themselves after Mary had brought them the incredible news that Jesus was alive. When they got to the tomb, they stooped down, looked in, and saw the linen bandages that had been wound around Jesus's body, inter-twined with spices (the Eastern way of burial) lying wrapped up . . . but with nobody inside. They saw the turban that had been wound around his head "not lying with the linen cloths but rolled up in a place by itself" (John 20:7). At that point, we read, they saw and believed. Why? Because it was apparent to them that the body of Jesus had emerged from those grave cloths, just as a butterfly emerges from its chrysalis; and the turban lay apart, just like the cap of a chrysalis case when the butterfly has come out. Incidentally, this has something to say about the modern suggestion that the resurrection of Jesus was somehow real but not physical. That seems to me rather like trying to have your cake and eat it too. To be sure, Christians have never held that the resurrection of Jesus was the mere resuscitation of a corpse. The New Testament proclaims that he was raised to a life of a new quality. Just like the butterfly, in fact. It does not emerge unchanged from when it went into that chrysalis. No, it is transformed to a new dimension of living. No longer is it a caterpillar, which crawls slowly and painfully wherever it wants to go. Now it can sail through the air with delicacy and poise. It is transformed into a new life. But it is unquestionably the same insect, despite the change brought about by its hibernation in the chrysalis. So it was with Jesus. His tomb was empty not in order to let him out but to let people in to see that he had indeed risen. The empty tomb and the empty grave cloths are symbols, pointers, to the fact that Jesus, the man, has become Christ, the risen Lord. "He holds the keys of death and of the afterlife," sang the prophet who wrote the book of Revelation (see 1:18). The person was indeed dead. But the tomb was found empty because death could not hold him. And that, as Peter said on the first day of Pentecost, was a remarkable fulfillment of a prophecy made a thousand years before:

> David says concerning him [Jesus], "...Thou wilt not abandon my soul to Hades, nor let thy Holy One see corruption. Thou has made known to me the ways of life...." Brethren, I may say to you confidently of the patriarch David that he both died and was

buried, and his tomb is with us to this day. Being therefore a prophet ... he foresaw ... the resurrection of the Christ, that he was not abandoned to Hades, nor did his flesh see corruption. This Jesus God raised up, and of that we are all witnesses.

Acts 2:25, 27–32

3. The church was born

In his penetrating study *The Phenomenon of the New Testament,* Professor C. F. D. Moule points out a remarkable thing about Christianity. It had absolutely nothing to add to Judaism, nothing whatsoever—except this conviction that the Rabbi Jesus had been raised from the dead! All the earliest Christians were loyal Jews, of course. They all went to the synagogue to worship. They read and believed the Jewish Scriptures. Their ethics were based on the Old Testament. Only one thing caused this new religion, as it emerged, to erupt. It was the conviction that Jesus must be the long-awaited deliverer from God, foretold in those Scriptures of the Old Testament, hinted at in all the sacrificial rituals of the Jewish people. He must be the Coming One; his resurrection from the dead proved it (Rom. 1:4). Nobody else had done that. Jesus was unique. No wonder they could do no less than give him the title "Lord," the name usually applied to the almighty God in the Old Testament Scriptures.

That church, armed with such an improbable claim, swept across the whole Roman Empire inside three hundred years. It is a perfectly amazing story of peaceful revolution, without parallel in the history of the world. It came about because Christians were able to say to unbelievers, "Jesus did not only die for you, but he is also alive. You can meet him and discover for yourself the reality we are talking about." People did discover for themselves. And the church, born out of the Easter grave, spread.

That church had three special characteristics. You found them everywhere it went. The Christians had a special day,

Sunday; a special rite of initiation, baptism; and a special meal, the Holy Communion. Now the interesting thing about these facts is this. Every one of the three is rooted in the resurrection of Jesus. Sunday, called "the Lord's Day" in Revelation 1:10, was given this remarkable name because it was the day, the first day of the week, on which the Lord Jesus rose from the tomb. The Jews had, from time immemorial, kept the seventh day of the week sacred. It recalled the completion of God's work of creation. Indeed, its observance was laid down in the Ten Commandments and remains one of the most distinguishing features of the Jewish nation. Yet these Jews who knew that Jesus was risen reckoned reasonably enough that God's new creation in the resurrection of Christ was even more memorable and significant than his act of creating the world in the first instance. It is quite something to change the day of rest after several thousand years. It needed nothing less than the resurrection to trigger it.

Then there was Christian baptism. You went down into a river, repenting of your sins and professing your faith in Jesus as Savior and Lord. You were immersed. You climbed out the other side. What did it mean? Simply this. That you, as a disciple, were linked to your Lord who went down into the dark river of death *and came up the other side.* It was an initiation ceremony that would have been unthinkable apart from the resurrection of Jesus.

It was just the same with the Lord's Supper, as they called it. This simple meal of bread and wine was shared by the Christians in memory of Jesus's body, broken (like the loaf) for them and his blood poured out (like the wine) for them. Understandable enough. But when the New Testament writers talk about this meal as an opportunity for exultant gladness, we can see that it is more than a memorial meal for a departed hero. They believed that the Lord who had died was alive and present in their midst. Death itself was conquered, and the conqueror was with them in all his risen power.

Baptism, communion, Sunday: all point to that resurrection of Jesus from the grave that acted as a launching pad—the only launching pad—for the whole Christian rocket that burst upon the ancient world.

4. The Lord appeared

Quite unmistakably. To lots of people. Paul gives a list of some of Jesus's appearances in 1 Corinthians 15, a letter he wrote about twenty years after the event, when plenty of eye-witnesses were still alive. Curiously enough he does not mention the appearance of Jesus to Mary of Magdala, though all the Gospels are clear that she was the first witness of the resurrection. Perhaps this was because no woman was considered a proper witness in either the Jewish or Gentile law in ancient society. Incidentally, if Christians had dreamed up the story of the empty tomb, would they have been stupid enough to attribute the discovery of that tomb and the first sight of the risen Jesus to a woman, whose testimony was legally worthless? That fact alone speaks volumes for the truth of the resurrection story. Although there were plenty of men who saw him later, it was to a despised woman that Jesus first appeared. Somehow it seems typical of him.

Let's glance at this list of witnesses that Paul brings us in 1 Corinthians 15. "I delivered to you as of first importance what I also received" (v. 3), he says to the people of Corinth—incidentally, using the words "delivered" and "received" in their technical sense of passing on duly authorized facts. What did he pass on?

> Christ died for our sins in accordance with the scriptures, . . . he was buried, . . . he was raised on the third day in accordance with the scriptures, and . . . he appeared.
>
> 1 Corinthians 15:3–5

To whom? First in the list he mentions Peter, the Peter who had denied him, then "the Twelve," presumably excluding Judas (dead) and Thomas (absent). Then he appeared to more than five hundred Christians at once, probably in Galilee where the majority of his followers lived. "Most of them are still alive," adds Paul, as if to say, "You can go and check up on the resurrection with them if you like." Jesus then appeared to James, his brother. He appeared to "all the apostles," presumably including Thomas this time. He appeared also to Paul. Now add to that group women, fishermen, a skeptical brother, a fanatical Pharisee opponent, and five hundred ordinary folk. Can any theory of hallucination cover those appearances? Hallucinations tend to happen to particular types of people—no one type here. Hallucinations tend to be allied with wish fulfillment—none of that here. Hallucinations tend to recur. These appearances ended after forty days and never came again. Hallucinations belong to the sick world—and it is hard to maintain that there was anything sick about these early missionaries as they preached the full health and salvation that their risen Messiah brought them. No, these appearances of the risen Christ are without parallel in the religious history of humankind. Nowhere else do you find anybody, still less so great a diversity of people, claiming to have had intimate personal contact (even to go as far as eating fish and honeycomb) with a much-loved leader recently killed. And it will not do to suppose that these were mere subjective visions. At least one of the apostles, Paul, was accustomed to having visions, was proud of them, and was very sure that this appearance of the Risen One was no vision (see 1 Cor. 9:1; 2 Cor. 12:1–7). It was a real encounter with Jesus after his resurrection.

5. Their lives were changed . . .

This has always been one of the strongest proofs of the truth of the resurrection. Those who claim to have come in contact with the risen Christ have had their lives transformed. Think of that list we looked at just now. Peter was changed from a coward who denied and forsook his Master, when the crunch came, into a man of rock whom the establishment could not cow by threats of imprisonment or death. Think of the Twelve, who were transformed from defeatists into a task force by the resurrection; theirs is one of the greatest "comeback" stories in the world. The five hundred were changed from a rabble into a church. All the apostles, including Thomas, came from unbelief to ardent faith. James, Jesus's skeptical brother, becomes suddenly changed into a believer and, more, becomes the leader of the Jerusalem church. What accounts for it? Simple: "he appeared to James." And perhaps most amazing of all is the about-face of Saul of Tarsus, the violent, bigoted persecutor of the Christians, who became the greatest follower Jesus ever had. The reason? "Last of all . . . he appeared . . . to me" (1 Cor. 15:8).

. . . and still are

But that first-century stuff is only half the story, remarkable though it is. It is not quite the same since those days, because nobody has seen the risen Lord with his own eyes. I imagine that Jesus displayed himself openly to his followers, allowed them to feel the holes in his hands and feet, even ate meals with them, in order to persuade them that he was still the Jesus they had known. Yet he passed through doors, disappeared while they were talking with him, and eventually parted from them for the last time on the Mount of Olives in order to persuade them that he had risen not just to a further span of life but to a new quality of life. From then on he would not appear to their physical eyes. But by his Spirit (no longer restricted to the confines of a physical body), he would indwell the very lives of his people, not just be alongside them, as he had during his time on earth. And that is what he has been doing ever since. So although we cannot say, like the first witnesses, "I have seen the Lord," every genuine Christian can say, "I know him. He has come into my life. He has made such radical changes that I cannot believe I am deluding myself." Every believer is, in this sense, a witness to the resurrection.

This, to me, was the most impressive demonstration of the truth that Jesus is alive. Before I became a Christian, I watched the lives of Christians for the best part of a year, and I discovered them to be different—different from my own life, and different from what they had been. I was once having a discussion with a number of postgraduate scientists, and you can imagine the number of objections to Christianity that were coming forward. And then one of the agnostics said simply, "I know there must be something in it because of the difference it has made to my friends."

The life-changing work of the risen Jesus goes on today, and it is a powerful testimony to the truth that he is indeed alive and well. I have been a Christian long enough now to be sure that I am not deluding myself. I have seen Christ's transforming touch change obviously needy characters, like long-term prisoners, compulsive gamblers and alcoholics, drug addicts, and prostitutes. I am just as moved by the way he changes the attitudes and the characters of more ordinary people. I think of a brilliant athlete I met, who also had a brilliant political career ahead of him. He was intensely ambitious. But, when he became a Christian, he decided that his games were to be used as a talent from God, and that his political career was in the Master's hands, to be used for his glory, not the satisfaction of his own ambition. The peace, the relaxation that came to him through allowing the Risen One to take over, was remarkable. His friends noticed it.

Or I think of an Oxford student I know. I met her first in church, when she was wrestling against the Christ she had become convinced was real. It was a long and tearful fight. Eventually she gave in. She developed not only a very different character—more gracious, more outgoing, more thoughtful of others—but she gave up two weeks of her vacation to go on a missions trip, sharing with others the discovery she herself had made. No matter whether it is in a spectacular conversion, or far more gentle ways, the risen Christ shines through his present-day witnesses. It reminds me a bit of the ending of *Godspell*. In this musical the joy of the resurrection is shown through dance. And members of the audience are invited to come up onto the stage and dance with the cast. They do not thereby become the cast, but they share the same experience. Now the cast, so to speak, is the first generation of disciples: Peter, James, and John, and others who saw the risen Christ. We cannot join the cast of eyewitnesses. But we can join them in the dance of Christian experience if we have come to know the living Lord.

The implications

Those, then, are five pieces of evidence. Together they point to one conclusion, that Jesus of Nazareth did not only die but also rose to a new life, an endless life, which enables him to meet and transform character today—your character, even—just as he did in the first century. We can be confident that Jesus pioneered the way through death, just as those first astronauts pioneered the way to the moon. And just as they brought back evidence about what lay on the hidden side of the moon, so he has shown what lies on the hidden side of death. Death is not the end. It is, or it can be, the gateway into a new quality of life, "butterfly life" instead of "caterpillar life."

If this is the case, we would be wise to listen very carefully to what this pioneer Jesus has to say about the hidden side of death. He ought to know. He has been there. He is very explicit. "Let not your hearts be troubled," he says to his disciples, who are grief-stricken at the prospect of his death. "Believe in God, believe also in me. In my Father's house are many rooms; if it were not so, would I have told you that I go to prepare a place for you?" (John 14:1–2). Those are words we can trust. They come from the one person who has broken the death barrier, the one person equipped to take other colonists with him to that uncharted land.

But there is another side of the coin. It is true that Christians can be confident that God will not scrap them at death. It is true they can rest with assurance on this promise of Jesus. They can look forward to death not as the end but as the end of the caterpillar stage. But what of those who are not linked to the Risen One? How can they hope to fare? Not very well, obviously. I should not fare very well if I tried to get to the moon under my own steam, however much hardware and rocketry was put at my disposal. I should need the skilled direction of an astronaut who had done it before. Without that, I should not stand a chance. That is why Jesus said to people who turned their backs on him,

> I am going away, and you will look for me, and you will die in your sin. Where I go, you cannot come.
>
> John 8:21 NIV

Does that sound hard? Not really. You cannot get to the moon unless you commit yourself to the astronaut. It is very sad, though. Jesus grieved over people who turned down his offer of life abundant, life forever. "You refuse to come to me that you may have life" (John 5:40). Curiously enough, the practical answer to the riddle of whether or not there is a life beyond the grave lies with us. We may choose whether we rot when we die or whether death becomes for us the chrysalis case to usher in a new quality of life with the Risen One.

13

"You can't change human nature."

By and large, you can't change human nature. That is why the early years are so important. The influence of home and school, of the first years in a job or time at college, tend to form our main characteristics. They will change, to some extent, with fresh opportunities, new pressures, responsibility (or lack of it), and age. But once the direction of a person's life and character are set, you do not find that rapid changes of character and attitude occur very often. You have only to think of the married couple whose years of living with one another enable them to predict with painful accuracy how the partner will react, even what the other will say, in a given situation. Or think of the person who comes out of prison, only to return there again for a similar offense. The leopard does not very often change its spots. You can indeed train up a young tree, or a young dog for that matter, in the direction that you want. But try bending a mature tree, try training a five-year-old dog, and you will be in for disappointment.

The Russian dissident Aleksandr Solzhenitsyn put the problem with his customary clarity: "Human nature changes not much faster than the geological face of the earth."[52] Indeed, the irony and the tragedy of modern life lies in this: we have become masters of our environment to a large degree, but we cannot produce any comparable control over ourselves.

52. Joseph Pearce, *Solzhenitsyn: A Soul in Exile* (HarperCollins, 2000).

We can alter environment but not people. But of course, we have had a good try.

Possible remedies?

Political change and social change have been two greatly favored avenues of improvement. Give people better education, improve their housing, and all will be well. Although, as a Christian, I am committed to these concerns, it can scarcely be argued that the result has lived up to the expectation. In Britain, the United States, and a host of other "educated" countries, the misery caused by violent crime, child sexual abuse, and racist attacks is rising each and every year. Washington, D.C., capital of free America, is almost at a crisis point over drug-related murders. Britain, Australia, and other developed nations have their own pressing problems. In our big cities, it can be lethal to walk home at night. In our opulent world, millions still die of starvation and preventable disease.

For followers of various brands of New Age thinking, the remedy for human nature lies in achieving a pattern of "inner coherence." They say that the self is kingpin, god in fact, and reality is whatever the god within accepts it to be. Considering this view of the world, James Sire suggests a way "to try to shock out of their delusion those who suppose themselves to be god." Following their logic, they are so wrapped up in their own universe that "pouring a pot of hot tea on their heads should produce no particular response. Still it might be worth a try!"[53]

But whatever we pursue, from new schools to the New Age, the problem is indeed intractable.

Look at unhappiness in the labor forces of the world, due to rival policies of greed and lack of job satisfaction. Look at

53. James Sire, *Why Should Anyone Believe Anything At All?* (Inter-Varsity Press, 1994).

unhappiness in so many homes, due to various brands of selfishness. Look at the tense relationships between many nations, due to rival policies of threat and hate. Look at the ecological situation, with its ruthless pursuance of short-term goals and neglect of future generations. Wherever you look, you see the ravages of the "human disease." We have all been infected by it. We do not have to learn to go wrong, though we do have to learn, painfully and slowly, to go right. To steal and lie, to clamor for our own way, to hate and lust, to be greedy and selfish are not imported products. They grow here, in you and me. And they grow with the perverse fecundity of weeds in our gardens; they need no planting, no watering, no care— whereas the flowers have to be cosseted and looked after with tender, loving care if they are to survive, let alone bloom. The human disease is like that very troublesome weed, ground elder. The more you pull it up, the more it seems to grow. Leave one particle of root in the soil, and it produces a fertile crop of the weed in next to no time. Nothing seems able to eradicate it. And it is the same with the human disease. Nothing seems able to eradicate it, and so we give up trying and say, "You can't change human nature."

Disastrous remedies?

Of course, some things *can* change it. Brain operations can do this and alter the personality of the patient beyond recognition. Brainwashing can, so much so that the captive can be trained actually to think like the captor. And perhaps disaster can. There are instances where the death of a close relative or the collapse of a love affair has changed a person's personality and whole outlook on life enormously. But all three of these possibilities—disaster, brainwashing, and brain surgery—we instinctively class as bad things. The cure is worse than the disease. If human nature can only be changed at the dictates of brain surgeons with their scalpels, brainwashers with their instruments of refined torture, and personal disasters, it is a pretty grim lookout. For all practical purposes, we can say again, "You can't change human nature."

There is nothing new about this conclusion. Thinkers and poets all through the ages have recognized it. Herodotus, the father of history, commented on it. Plato, the greatest philosopher there has ever been, discovered the hard truth of it when he tried to educate the tyrant of Syracuse. For all his educative theory and unsurpassed skill as a teacher, Plato failed miserably and was ejected for his pains by that unpleasant youth. Ovid, the poet, banished by the Emperor Augustus for his eroticism, combined realism and humor as he wrote, "I see the better course, and I approve of it; but I follow the worse." Those words were echoed by his contemporary, the apostle Paul. He spoke of the miserable human condition that he shared. He put it something like this in one of his letters: "I don't understand myself at all, for I really want to do what is right, but I can't. I do what I don't want to—what I hate. I ... know I am rotten through and through, as far as my old sinful nature is concerned. No matter which way I turn, I can't make myself do right. I want to, but I can't. I want to do good, but when I try not to do wrong, I do it anyway" (see Rom. 7:18–20).

Doesn't that first-century rabbi speak to your condition? Isn't it just like that with you? It is with me. Very well, then, might it not be worth listening to his momentous claim, since his analysis of our human disease is so convincing? His claim is simply this: there is a cure. He had found it and applied it and discovered that it did change his human nature, but in a way far different from the grim effects of the brain surgery, the brainwashing, and the disasters we have considered. As you would expect with this redoubtable opponent of the Man of Nazareth, who became Jesus's foremost apostle and preacher, this cure-all centers around Jesus. May I recap a little at this stage in the book?

Effective remedy?

We have seen that the really conclusive answer to whether there is a God or not is Jesus Christ. He embodies the God we cannot see in terms we can understand—human terms. He brings us all of God we could take in. He was not just a good man; he was God himself, joining his nature to ours and coming to the floor of our factory, so to speak. All religions point to a dimension higher than our own. All have within them some search for the truth. All possess some elements of the light, which has taken full and final form in the Light of the World, Jesus Christ himself. So God himself has met one of our basic needs, to know about him. He has come to show us.

We have another basic need, to get right with this God who has demonstrated in Jesus his loveliness of character, his goodness and fierce hatred of evil. If God is Christlike, it is very plain that I am not. And there lies a problem. We considered it in chapter 10. No good deeds from me, no payment, no religious activities could span the yawning gulf between the Lord's goodness and—let's be frank about it—my badness. This problem was so acute that it led to the cross. It directed Jesus inexorably to the place where he laid down his life for ours, where he took responsibility for all man's evil in the sight of God. Such was God's generosity that Jesus did not merely come to show us what he was like, but he died that most agonizing death to reconcile us and enable anyone who was prepared to say, "God be merciful to me, a sinner," to enjoy his company here on earth, and also hereafter. This is one of the important sides to the resurrection that we considered in chapter 12.

All these things Paul writes about in his letters, which are preserved in our New Testament. He rejoices in them; he is thrilled by them. He is completely taken up in loving adoration of and service to the God who makes them available. But there is one other side in this all-embracing rescue that God has done for us, which thrills Paul almost more than any of the others. It is this: God has found a way to change human nature.

The Spirit of Jesus

Briefly, what it amounts to is this. He is willing not just to reveal himself to us, nor merely to die for us. He is actually prepared to come and live in us. Now if that sounds stupid, wait a moment. We get somewhere near it when, in ordinary speech, we say, "Stalin had the spirit of Hitler in him," or "Jimmy is a proper Don Juan." We mean that the sort of qualities found in Hitler or Don Juan are reproduced in Stalin or Jimmy. Well, that includes what Christians mean when they speak of Christ's Spirit coming to live in them. We mean that the same characteristics that were seen in Jesus begin to make their appearance in the lives of his followers. Paul put it like this:

> When the Holy Spirit controls our lives, he will produce this kind of fruit in us: love, joy, peace, patience, kindness, goodness, faith-fulness, gentleness and self-control.
>
> Galatians 5:22–23 NLT

But Christians mean a lot more than this. We mean that this Jesus, who died and rose, is not a spent force. He is alive and well. When he was in Palestine, he was limited in what he could do and where he could be. If he was talking to me here, he could not be talking to you there. Such are the limitations of the human body. But shortly before his death, Jesus told his followers that it would be a good thing for them if he went away; if he did not, the Spirit would not become available to them. If he did go, however, he would send the Spirit in his place to make his presence real to them. And that was precisely what they experienced.

It all began on the day of Pentecost, just fifty days after the crucifixion of Jesus Christ at Passover time. To their amaze-ment they had, many of them, seen the risen Jesus during those intervening weeks. They had become convinced that he was

vibrantly alive. The Risen One told them that these appearances of his were only temporary, and that as a permanent gift
his Spirit would come and indwell their very personalities.
They did not understand what he meant, despite Old Testament Scriptures, which spoke of God putting his Spirit within
his followers and enabling them each to know him and to walk
in his ways. But after their experience on the day of Pentecost,
they knew for sure. They had a living experience of the Spirit
of Jesus, not merely influencing them from outside but coming
to grow the lovely flowers of his character in the barren soil of
their own lives. They were, quite literally, born into a new
dimension of experience, as a fetus is when it struggles through
the birth canal and draws its first breath, or as a woman and
man are the day they get married, or as a larva is the day it turns
into a dragonfly. The natural world does prepare us, just a little,
for the truth that human nature can be changed by the renew-
ing power of the Holy Spirit of God, once he is accepted into
our lives. And this realization gives the Christian something to
sing about. After that heartrending cry of defeat from Paul the
unaided human being, which we saw above, Paul the Christian
can proclaim triumphantly, "There is now no condemnation
awaiting those who belong to Christ Jesus. For the power of
the life-giving Spirit—and this power is mine through Jesus
Christ—has freed me from the vicious circle of sin and
death.... So now we can obey God's laws if we are led by the
Holy Spirit and no longer obey the old evil nature with us"
(a paraphrase of Rom. 8:1–4).

In the remainder of this chapter, I propose to glance at ten
practical examples, taken from the pages of the New Testament
or from contemporary experience, of what the Holy Spirit can
do in a person, once he is given control.

1. Changed attitudes

First, the Spirit of Jesus can change your inner attitudes. I can't
combat my own deep-seated prejudices. But the Spirit of the

God who made me, and died to reconcile me, can do just that. I remember a saintly missionary, Bishop Don Jacobs, telling of a dream he had shortly after beginning work as a white person in a black African area. He still retained some illusions about white superiority, and his work was, not unnaturally, hampered by this. In the dream he saw himself on a hot day standing by a river in which many native people were washing themselves. "Go and bathe, Don," the Lord's Spirit seemed to be saying to him. "Not beneath all those folk, Lord," was his instinctive response. "I'll swim upstream of them." And then he saw in his dream that the river welled out from the cross of Calvary. There was no room for pride of place there. So he gladly immersed himself in that river, downstream of his African brethren, and on that day the Spirit of God dealt with his inbred arrogance. Thereafter, for many years of loving ministry among African peoples, there was no hint of pride in his dealings with them. He was a new person; his very attitudes had been changed.

2. Lifestyle changed

Second, the Spirit of Jesus can change your whole way of life. It may or may not have been socially acceptable previously, but it needed attention. I think of two eminently respectable people: a mother of four and a leading civil official. The mother's sharpness with the children and her less-than-kind gossip have changed radically; people wonder what has happened to her. The official's attitude to his subordinates, once overbearing, is now gracious; his love of money has been taken away, and he now sees his possessions as a trust to use for God. But I think also of one not so respectable—a hospital porter who came to Christ at much the same time as these two. He had committed a long list of crimes that had never been detected. What did the Spirit of God prompt him to do? Something that he would never have dreamed of doing of his own accord: to go and confess his crimes to the police. This he did—and they were very surprised! In both "respectable" and "unacceptable," the Spirit of Christ was changing lifestyles.

The delightful thing about this transformation is that it is basically the same wherever men and women come to Christ. The Spirit of the risen Lord begins to change their lives for the better and gradually makes them more like Christ. It was the same way in the first days of the church. Think of those disciples who wanted to burn down a Samaritan village just because they got a cold welcome there in the days that Jesus was with them. A few years later, after they had received his Spirit into their lives, they were spreading the gospel of love and forgiveness to those same Samaritans. Some of the earliest converts, the Thessalonians, who turned from idols to the true God, showed it by the way they lived; Paul can commend them on their increase in faith and love, the holiness that was replacing lust, the humility that replaced their traditional Macedonian arrogance, and their patience in suffering and persecution.

3. Habits broken

Third, the Spirit of Jesus can break long-standing habits. Of course he can. Jesus was never bound by habits he could not control, and "where the Spirit of the Lord is, there is freedom" (2 Cor. 3:17). A friend of mine has been inside many of the reformatories and prisons in England for stealing cars. He found Christ while serving a sentence in one of those prisons and has never been back. His philosophy of "Get from no matter whom" has changed to "Give to no matter whom," and he is now in the ordained ministry of the Church of England. He does not have much money now, but he is content. Like the apostle Paul of old, he has found that the life-giving power of the Spirit of Jesus has set him free from the vicious circle of the old ways.

This sort of thing is not the exception once the Spirit of Christ gets inside a person; it becomes the rule. I think of an obsessive gambler set free from his craze to gamble. I think of chain-smokers, knowing their habit to be harmful but unable to break it, who welcomed the Spirit of Christ into their lives and discovered the reality of his power to break the habit. I think of folks who could scarcely utter a sentence without an oath, whose long-standing habit was broken by the Spirit of Jesus. It is not only with famous people and great sins that the Spirit of Jesus can help. The Spirit, endued with all the power of the risen Lord Jesus, is meant for *you*.

4. Love for hate

Fourth, the Spirit of Jesus can replace hate by love. Hate is one of the two most powerful human emotions, and love is the other. In some ways they are very near to one another, so that a lover, once jilted, can passionately hate the person he or she once loved, but you don't very often find it happening the other way around. But the Spirit of Jesus makes a habit of it. In the days of apartheid, I have seen the faces of black South Africans filled with joy and love for white Christians, who belong to the race of those who have oppressed them. I have seen Christian believers in Ireland loving and caring for one another across the traditional "Catholic" and "Protestant" divide. I have seen Christian believers from the Masai and Kikuyu tribes, among the most hostile in all Africa, loving and serving one another. I have seen the same thing in Jerusalem, with Christian believers from the Arab and Jewish races living together in love and mutual commitment. Jesus produces that sort of change in human lives. I think of the love of those missionaries who, in the late 1950s, went to try to evangelize the savage Stone Age tribe of the Aucas in South America and got speared to death for their pains. Their wives and sisters devoted themselves to the same task and saw such fruit from their work that the majority of this small tribe turned to Jesus Christ. One of the tribesmen, who had himself killed one of the original missionaries, toured England some years later with the wife of the man he had killed; both of them not only taught but also demonstrated that the

Spirit of Jesus had replaced hatred with love. Love is the greatest thing in the world. We need it badly these days, and the Spirit of Jesus can supply it in unlimited measure: "God's love has been poured into our hearts through the Holy Spirit which has been given to us" (Rom. 5:5).

5. A mind enlightened

Fifth, the Spirit of Jesus can renew your mind. My job for many years has been in theological education. I have seen people who have failed every exam and been thrown out of school at fifteen not only equip themselves for the intellectually demanding work of the ordained ministry but in many cases get a degree as well. If this had occurred once or twice, it would have been remarkable. But it has happened every year. Once the Spirit of Christ takes over the personality, he opens up all sorts of doors; the mental door is one of them. I believe that the Spirit enlivens our intellectual faculties, enabling us to see truth in a way we had been blind to before. And by this I do not mean merely spiritual truth, as though such a thing existed. All truth is God's truth, and once the Spirit of truth enters a person's soul, we ought not to be surprised if his or her capacity for truth and knowledge grows. I think of an ex-colleague of mine whom I had taught in earlier days. He had left school at fifteen, entirely unqualified. He found Christ shortly afterward, and thereafter the growth of his personality, not least on the intellectual side, began. He began educating himself, gained entry to college, got a good degree, followed it with a Masters in Theology and a Ph.D., and has become an author, a university teacher, a theological college principal, and a minister in the heart of a great university city. To top it all off, he became the Archbishop of Canterbury! That is perhaps the most out-standing example I know of for what the Spirit of God is constantly doing: opening blind eyes to the truth. The Spirit of life invariably enlivens our perceptions. Augustine found that. He held out long enough against the Spirit of God, but eventually he gave in, and his mind, as well as his heart, was captivated and renewed by the Spirit of the Lord. It can happen with you. You will not necessarily become an Augustine, but you will find your insight deepened and your capacity to read, understand, and learn enhanced.

6. A body renewed

Sixth, the Spirit of Jesus can change your bodily health. I wish to be careful here because many false claims are made on this score. Instant healing is as suspect as most other "instant" products of our impatient world. Moreover, it is clear that the Spirit of Jesus does not always heal a man or woman physically. Even in the days of Jesus and the apostles, not everyone who came to them with illnesses was healed. In some cases, we are told it was because of their unbelief. Paul himself was not cured of an affliction he called his "thorn in the flesh," and we read of him leaving Trophimus at Miletus sick, and of Timothy with an unhealed stomach complaint. Nevertheless, God has the power to heal, and the pages of the Acts, as well as the Epistles, are full of examples of the healing work of his Spirit once he is allowed into a person's life. And isn't this just what you would expect? God is the author of all healing, whether "miraculous" or through normal medical means. Would it be all that surprising if he undertook major repairs in the body he was beginning to inhabit? After all, the New Testament makes it very plain that church buildings are not where we are to find the Holy Spirit but within people themselves: "Your body is a temple of the Holy Spirit" (1 Cor. 6:19). All over the world Christians are waking up to this long-neglected truth, that the Spirit of God can and does heal, not only non-organic diseases but also organic ones like cancer and blindness. I have been slow to admit this and have even written cautiously against it in a previous book, but I have now met so many people who have been healed, once they opened their lives to the Spirit, that I can only bemoan my previous unbelief and rejoice in the healing work that the Spirit of God does do in some cases reckoned incurable by the medical profession.

7. The conscience cleansed

Seventh, the Spirit of Jesus can cleanse the conscience. There is a lovely passage in the letter to the Hebrews that explains that the blood of Christ, that is to say his atoning death on the cross, when applied to the individual by the Holy Spirit, can cleanse the conscience (see Heb. 9:14). Now that is a marvelous thing. One eminent psychiatrist said that if his mental patients could have their accusing consciences stilled and be assured of forgiveness, half of his hospital beds would become empty at once. I think of a woman I know whose conscience deeply accused her for sleeping with a married man. She cared a lot about him and could not break it, but she knew it was wrong. Then she heard the good news of Jesus, his love, his pardon, and his ability to change people's lives. She surrendered her life to him. She poured out her heart in confession. She was absolutely sure of his pardon, for "if we confess our sins, he is faithful and just, and will forgive our sins and cleanse us from all unrighteousness" (1 John 1:9). The Spirit of God not only broke the power of that habit in her at one fell swoop, but he also gave her deep assurance in her inner being that Christ had dealt with her sin and that her conscience could no longer condemn her. That woman came with me some weeks later on ward rounds and began talking to patients about Jesus. Her joy, her confidence, and the manifest change in her life were wonderful to see. The Spirit of God assures us we belong; he gives an inner witness that God has accepted us into his family (see Rom. 8:16). And that is treasure indeed.

8. Sex life transformed

Eighth, the Spirit of Jesus can change your sexual life. This is an area that requires spring-cleaning in most of us. It did in the earliest Christians too. Paul is explicit on the point.

> Do not be deceived; neither the immoral, nor idolaters, nor adulterers, nor homosexuals … nor drunkards … will inherit the kingdom of God. And such were some of you. But you were washed, you were sanctified, you were justified in the name of the Lord Jesus Christ and in the Spirit of our God.
>
> 1 Corinthians 6:9–11

The lives of these immoral folk in Corinth had been transformed by the power of the Spirit entering their lives and setting them free. The same remains true today.

I think of a woman who had turned violently anti-Christian. The reason, I discovered, was because she had been sleeping with her boyfriend and found this incompatible with carrying on a Christian life. She came to rededicate her life and was willing to sleep with him no more until they got married. She was, however, very frightened of how he would react. But such is the generosity of God that he dealt with her boyfriend just as he had with her—her boyfriend allowed the Spirit of Christ to take control of his sex life, but he wondered what his girlfriend would say! You can imagine the joy with which they met and the new level at which their relationship continued. I still possess a delightful letter from them, telling me of the tremendous joy it brought them to surrender their relationship to the lordship of the Spirit and discover the moral power and the joy in self-discipline that he brought them.

Again, I think of several occasions when a marriage has been on the point of breaking up, and the Spirit of Christ has been welcomed into the hearts of both partners. The result has been staggering. No longer were they jaded with each other, no longer in search of fresh thrills with other partners. They had discovered a new bond of unity, undergirding the physical, legal, and mental unity that threatened to be insufficient to hold them together.

I had a letter from a homosexual. He had heard the gospel, rejected it, and had gone to live in a homosexual apartment. He had not been able to forget what he had heard about Jesus, however, and set himself to read the New Testament. What he found there, and the testimony of another Christian he came across, brought him to Christ. He surrendered his sexual urges to the Lord and found that he was able thereafter to have a normal heterosexual relationship. He is now happily married. I do not know whether this is possible in all cases of inversion. Very possibly not. But the Spirit of God, who can enable a heterosexually inclined person to live a pure single life, can also enable a homosexually inclined person not to indulge his appetites. Of that I am very sure. And the single life is no dead end. It enables you to do many things that a married person cannot do. See what Paul had to say about its advantages in 1 Corinthians 7. And remember that Jesus, the most balanced man who ever lived, remained single—*and fulfilled!* Do not believe the modern myth that nobody can be normal and fulfilled without overt sexual activity. That is a lie. If the Spirit of God calls you to a single life, he will so fulfill and satisfy you that you are thrilled with your lot and would not choose anything different if you could live your life all over again. Yes, the Spirit can and does make an enormous difference where our sexual drives are concerned.

9. Rescue from despair

Ninth, the Spirit of Jesus can change your despair. Maybe you haven't got any, but lots of people have, these days. Not just despair at the political, industrial, and moral chaos of our times but also the much deeper despair of living in a universe that seems to them to be random and purposeless. Jacques Monod put it well in his *Chance and Necessity* when he wrote, "Our number came up in the Monte Carlo game. Is it surprising that the person who has just made a million at the casino should feel strange and empty?"[54] Or, as Camus put it in his

54. Jacques Monod, *Chance and Necessity: Essay on the Natural Philosophy of Modern Biology* (Penguin, 1997).

Caligula, "What is intolerable is to see one's life drained of meaning, to be told there is no reason for existing. A man can't live without some reason for living."[55] The Holy Spirit gives just that reason for living, just that sense of purpose, which many of the most perceptive modern men and women are painfully aware that they lack. The New Testament writers spoke of "joy in the Holy Spirit," and they showed it in the quality of their lives. They certainly had something to exult about, and so have we. If your Creator sets such value on you that he died to reconcile you to himself and then comes to indwell your very life, that gives a fantastic sense of worth and purpose to your very existence. I remember being struck by this a few years ago when reading in a letter of the joy of some prisoners in a jail on Penang (an island of Malaysia) who had been brought to faith in Christ by a prison visitor before their execution. It shows with great clarity the sense of well-being, of purpose, of joy that the Spirit of Jesus brings into a life, even if that life faces almost immediate extinction on the human plane.

Our dear Rev. Khoo,

We do thank you from the bottom of our hearts ... for all you have done for us. You were everything in our hour of need. You were the beacon that guided us to the haven of Jesus Christ. You taught us to have unquestioning faith in God's Word, to pray to Him, and to ask for His forgiveness. During these long agonizing months of mental torture ... till now we stand at the very brink of death, at the very edge of eternity, you have given us so much of yourself in selfless devotion. It is through you that we now look death in the face with courage and calmness, for we doubt not God's promise of forgiveness by the simple act of belief and acceptance. We know that in three and one half hour's time when we pass from off this earth, our Lord and Savior Jesus Christ will be waiting with open arms to lead us to our new home in the

55. Albert Camus, *Caligula/Le Malentendu* (Editions Flammarion, 1997).

house of the Father.... With our dying breath we once again affirm to you our undying gratitude—gratitude that will transcend even death itself.

10. Character refined

Tenth, the Spirit of Jesus can make a new person out of you. The pages of the New Testament are full of examples of the transformation the Spirit of Jesus makes to the most unlikely characters once he is invited in. Think of the change in a top-ranking Roman governor like Sergius Paulus. Think of a vacillating, cowardly braggart like Simon Peter in the Gospels, who became the "rock" of the early church, fearless in the face of opposition, sleeping peacefully the night before his execution; that change was due to the Spirit. Think of a rabid opponent of Jesus like Saul of Tarsus, converted and changed beyond all recognition by the Spirit of the one he had persecuted and then come to love.

Perhaps, though, there is no more remarkable example of the way God's Spirit makes new men of people than the tiny one-page letter of Paul to Philemon. Philemon was a rich landowner, converted to Christ through Paul's ministry. He had a slave, Onesimus, who took his opportunity one day and ran off with a fair amount of Philemon's cash. By one of the humorous coincidences that God seems to delight in, Onesimus landed up in the same prison as Paul! You can guess what happened next. Paul led the man to Christ, and at once Onesimus's conscience started to work. Ought he not to go back to the master he had robbed? Yes, but Philemon would surely kill him, as owners were in a habit of doing to runaway slaves. So Paul wrote this little gem of a letter to the Christian landowner about his runaway and now Christian slave. He commends Onesimus not only to Philemon's forgiveness but also to his respect as a fellow human being and to his love as a fellow Christian. Now think of the revolution in those two characters, Philemon and Onesimus. It so happens that we have a papyrus fragment from roughly this time, coming from a slave owner whose slave had run away. The writer encourages the recipient to hunt down the man and kill him. Yet Philemon forgives his slave, respects his slave, and loves his slave like a brother! As for Onesimus, the last thing in the world he would normally do would be to go back to the landowner from whom he had escaped. Now that he had come to Christ and was beginning to be changed by his Spirit, his conscience awoke, and he was prepared to go back, risk death, offer reparations for what he had stolen, and live on as a slave in Philemon's employment. As a matter of fact, reading between the lines of Paul's letter to Philemon, we find a strong hint that Philemon should release the man and give him his freedom. I guess he did. And it may be mere coincidence, but we do find that the Christian bishop in that part of the world twenty years later was a man called Onesimus. . . .

That runaway slave reminds me of a modern half parallel. I know a man who went into the ordained ministry but who did not know the life-changing power of the Spirit of Jesus. He labored away for five years without any results, threw in his hand, and resigned from the ministry. He dropped out of conventional society. He became an unemployed thug, a slave to women, to drink, and to smoking. He was one of life's casualties. I had the joy of introducing that man to Christ. There was a group who loved and cared for him and sustained him in the early days. He came to train afresh in Britain before going back overseas to the ministry from which he had withdrawn. And God has given him particular gifts as an evangelist among the tough down-and-outs, the drug takers, the drunks, and the prostitutes whose scene he knows so well. Needless to say, the slavery to drink and tobacco has been broken and his whole character gradually transformed.

All his business
We may not be slaves and thieves like Onesimus. We may not be in bondage to alcoholism and promiscuity like my friend.

But in a sense we are all Onesimuses. We all have habits to which we are enslaved. We have learned to live with those habits, to be comfortable with them, to excuse them with the refrain, "Well, you can't change human nature." To that the Spirit of Jesus replies, "You can't be serious. Changing human nature is my business."

14

... to the Reader

If you have been with me thus far, where does this bring us? I began, you will recall, with a plea for honesty; to have done with excuses that come so unthinkingly to our lips as we evade the issue of God. We then looked at a series of these common responses about religion. It was clear that we cannot with integrity claim that we are not the religious kind, as if that would get us out of looking at the evidence. We went on to examine some of that evidence that made it much harder not to believe in God than to believe in him, while recognizing that you cannot actually prove personal existence of any kind, your own or God's. It became clear that although there are many true sayings preserved in many religions, and many impressive lives lived by their practitioners, it is neither logical nor possible to suppose that all religions lead to God. Indeed, there is more than a streak in human nature that does not want to know too much about God and is very keen to profess agnosticism about his existence, or at least to keep him at a distance; his closer presence would be altogether too demanding and uncomfortable. But his closer presence is just what we seem to have to face. Jesus confronts us with it. And it simply will not do to class Jesus Christ among the great prophets or the good men of the world. The old dilemma remains: he is either God or he is not good. No "good man" made the claims he did. No "good man" rose from the dead.

If, in Jesus, God himself has come to look for us, it clearly will not do to imagine that as long as we are sincere, it does not matter what we believe. Nor will doing our best solve our problems. Our best is manifestly not good enough for ourselves, let alone God. Even if we could keep the Ten Commandments and the Sermon on the Mount for the rest of our days, that would not change the past or erase its ugly blots. The more I know people, the more certain I am of the truth of the Bible's diagnosis: "The heart is deceitful above all things, and desperately corrupt" (Jer. 17:9). Everybody has a past that contains things of which they have good reason to be ashamed. And nothing can change the past; nothing, that is, if we leave out of the equation the death of Jesus, which puts sinful people like us in the clear with God. Had there been any other way, we can be sure God would have taken it, rather than allow Jesus to go to that grim cross. The cross, then, is very much the heart of Christianity; ours is a faith that has a gallows as its badge. On that gallows the most important battle of history was fought and won: Christ there suffered for sins, the righteous for the unrighteous, to bring us to God.

Nor was that all. Christians do not remember with gratitude a dead Christ. They rejoice in the companionship of a living Lord who rose from the grave and is alive today. This resurrection is as crucial to Christianity as is the cross. It means that there is a life after death. It means that Jesus can bring us there. It means his atoning death was sufficient to deal with a world's sin. It means his conquering presence is available to battle on against ingrained evil in his people. And this is where the Holy Spirit comes in. For, as we saw in the last chapter, the Spirit can be described as Jesus's "other self," the one who makes him real to believing people all over the world, and who works out in them the character of Jesus.

Such is God's provision for us, when really we had no claim on him at all. His generosity is breathtaking. What is to be done about it? May I make some simple suggestions?

New life

Reflect on this amazing fact, that he did this not just for the world or for the next person but for *you*. He loves you. He made you. He died for you. He waits to come and live in your life. You need his spring-cleaning. You need his pardon, his guidance, his joy, his sticking power, his courage in the face of death. These qualities are available to you, but only in Jesus Christ.

Is this, perhaps, the moment to kneel down and make your personal response to the love of God? "The gift of God is eternal life," says the New Testament (see Rom. 6:23). What do you do with a gift? You accept it gratefully. It is just the same with Jesus. He is God's great gift to you; all the other gifts are wrapped up in him. Do not duck the issue by waiting till you're good enough—you never will be. Just accept the gift thankfully, perhaps in words like these:

> O God, I am amazed at your generosity. I don't deserve it. I can hardly believe it. But I do dimly feel you are there, and I realize that you came to this earth for me in Jesus Christ. I do believe he died for my sins and is alive so that he can come by his Spirit into my heart. I realize that he wants to involve me in his ongoing work and among his people, and I am prepared for that. Lord, here and now I accept in faith the gift of Jesus to me personally. Please never allow me to go back on this decision, and please enable me to live worthy of it in your strength, wherever future circumstances take me.

New lifestyle

Having taken this momentous step, tell someone about it. Do this for two important reasons. One, it puts you into contact with others who can help you in the early days of your discipleship. Two, it enables you to nail your colors to the mast, and the New Testament is insistent on the need for this: "If you confess with your mouth, 'Jesus is Lord,' and believe in your heart that God raised him from the dead, you will be saved" (Rom. 10:9 NIV).

Of course, this will involve in due course letting "your light so shine before men, that they may see your good works and give glory to your Father who is in heaven" (Matt. 5:16). But it may be as well to start with Christians first, before going to tell the toughest atheist you know that you have surrendered your life to Jesus Christ! At all events, open unashamed discipleship is called for. Secret disciples rarely grow.

Next, it would be a good idea to read something on the basic essentials of Christian living, so as to have, as it were, a bird's-eye view of what it will involve. If you have almost no time, read J. R. W. Stott's booklet *Being a Christian* (Inter-Varsity Press). If you have a bit more time, read my own book, *New Life, New Lifestyle* (Hodder & Stoughton) or John White's *The Fight* (Inter-Varsity Press). In this way you will quickly get some ideas about continuing in the companionship of the one you have begun to trust.

Third, it is most important to get involved in Christian fellowship. The church, for all its failings, is not a luxury but a necessity. Jesus did not just come to save individuals but to set up on earth a first installment of the kingdom of God. And that means a society. You cannot get away from it. From now on your lot is cast with the Christian church. Where it is corrupt, purge it. Where it is slack, enliven it. Where it is right, follow it. But join it you must. So if you are not baptized, it is high time to seek out a minister in some lively church who will prepare you for baptism. If your denomination baptizes infants, you may well already be baptized. In that case, you will want to get confirmed, or the equivalent method of entry into full membership, so that you can pull your weight in the local congregation, take part in the Holy Communion, and give public testimony to your allegiance to Christ.

Next, may I pass on a piece of advice that I found invaluable in the early days of following Christ? Is there some Christian friend whom you know well? If so, he or she will be able to help you a great deal if you meet him or her regularly, not only socially but in order to read a bit of the Bible together, to talk over any difficulties as they occur, and to learn from him or her how to engage in real prayer (as opposed to the bedside noises you may have uttered for a long time without developing them at all). I had, for some months, a weekly session with such a friend, and it made all the difference.

Finally, get involved in some area of Christian service. It does not much matter what it is as long as you do it for Jesus' sake and to help other people. Pray to be guided to the contribution you could best make. But do something. Don't be a drone in the Christian hive, sucking up the honey and doing none of the work. Christian service is one of the great ways of growing to maturity in the Christian life.

Well, there it is. That would be this author's hope for his readers. I am sure that if you commit yourself realistically and wholeheartedly to God in this way, you will cease to produce the parrot cries that may have satisfied you up till now ("All religions lead to God," "It doesn't matter what you believe as long as you are sincere," and the rest). Instead you will begin to produce the cries of the newly born child of God as the Spirit gets to work within you, enabling you to cry, "Abba, dear Father."

Further Reading

For those who wish to examine some issues in greater depth.

About God

Packer, James. *Knowing God*. London: Hodder & Stoughton, 1975.

Watson, David. *Is Anyone There?* London: Hodder & Stoughton, 1979.

Williams, Peter S. *The Case for God*. London: Monarch, 1999.

About alternatives to Christian belief

Anderson, Sir Norman. *Christianity and World Religions: The Challenge of Pluralism*. Leicester, England: Inter-Varsity Press, 1984.

Green, Michael. *But Don't All Religions Lead to God?* Tonbridge, Kent, England: Sovereign World, 2002.

McGrath, Alister E. *The Twilight of Atheism*. New York: Doubleday Books, 2004.

Neill, Stephen. *Christian Faith and Other Faiths*. New York: Oxford University Press, 1960.

Sire, James W. *The Universe Next Door*. Leicester, England: Inter-Varsity Press, 1988.

About suffering

Eareckson, Joni. *A Step Further*. Basingstoke, England: Pickering & Inglis, 1979.

Kreeft, Peter. *Making Sense out of Suffering*. London: Hodder & Stoughton, 1987.

Lewis, C. S. *The Problem of Pain*. London: Collins Fount, 1962.

Needham, David. *How Could God Let This Happen?* Leicester, England: Inter-Varsity Press, 1989.

About science

Barton, Andrew. *Questions of Science*. Eastbourne, England: Kingsway, 1999.

Polkinghorne, John. *The Way the World Is*. London: SPCK, 1983.

About Christian evidence

Chapman, Colin. *Christianity on Trial*. Oxford: Lion Publishing, 1988.

McGrath, Alister E. *The Twilight of Atheism*. New York: Doubleday Books, 2004.

About Jesus

The Gospels (in a modern translation).

Green, Michael. *Who Is This Jesus?* London: Kingsway, 2004.

John, J. *The Life: A Portrait of Jesus*. London: Authentic Lifestyle, 2003.

About the cross and resurrection

Green, Michael. *The Empty Cross of Jesus*. London: Kingsway, 2004.

Stott, John. *The Cross of Christ*. Leicester, England: Inter-Varsity Press, 1989.

About the Holy Spirit and prayer

Green, Michael. *I Believe in the Holy Spirit*. London: Kingsway, 2003.

Holloway, Jane. *Prayer for Amateurs*. London: Hodder &
    Stoughton, 2000.
Huggett, Joyce. *Listening to God*. London: Hodder &
    Stoughton, 1986.
Magdalen, Sister Margaret. *Jesus—Man of Prayer*. London:
    Hodder & Stoughton, 1987.

Michael Green is one of the world's leading evangelists and is Senior Research Fellow at Wycliffe Hall, where he teaches on evangelism and New Testament studies. Michael has served as Principal of St. John's College, Nottingham; Rector of St. Aldate's Church, Oxford; Professor of evangelism at Regent College, Vancouver; and Advisor to the archbishops of Canterbury and York on evangelism. He is the author of numerous books on evangelism and the Christian faith.

More great tools for sharing your faith without fear

It could be the most important conversation you have with a loved one, and you don't want to risk pushing them away. Michael Green can help you navigate the potentially hazardous waters when sharing your faith with the ones closest to your heart.

talking about Jesus without offending

sharing your faith
with friends and family

Michael Green

MICHAEL GREEN

"BUT DON'T ALL RELIGIONS LEAD TO GOD?"

NAVIGATING *the* MULTI-FAITH MAZE

More likely than not, you've heard someone insist that sincere belief is what gets you to heaven, no matter what you put your faith in. Nothing could be further from the truth. Get the answers you need to help the religious pluralists in your life see the light.